RELIGION IN BALI

INSTITUTE OF RELIGIOUS ICONOGRAPHY
STATE UNIVERSITY GRONINGEN

ICONOGRAPHY OF RELIGIONS

EDITED BY

TH. P. VAN BAAREN, L. LEERTOUWER and H. BUNING (*Secretary*)

SECTION XIII: INDIAN RELIGIONS

FASCICLE TEN

LEIDEN
E. J. BRILL
1973

RELIGION IN BALI

BY

C. HOOYKAAS

With 48 Plates

LEIDEN
E. J. BRILL
1973

ISBN 90 04 03797 7

PRINTED IN THE NETHERLANDS

CONTENTS

ACKNOWLEDGEMENTS

First of all I thank my wife who from the outset encouraged me and advised me.

In the field of photography I received help from:

Drs. P. L. Dronkers, Eindhoven: a, b 1.
Prof. Dr. J. Ensink, University of Groningen: n 1, n 2.
Mrs. Drs. Hedi Hinzler, Kern Institute, Leiden. d 2, m 2, u 1-5, w 1, w 2, x 2, x 3.
Mr. Mark Hobart, M. A. University of London: k 1, k 4, o 4, o 5.
Mrs. Drs. C. M. C. Hooykaas-van Leeuwen Boomkamp: g 3, k 2, k 3, m 3, o 1, o 2, p 1-3, q 1-5, t 2, t 5, v 1-4, w 3-4, x 1, x 4.
Koninklijk Instituut voor Taal-, Land- en Volkenkunde, Leiden: f 1.
(Gedong) Kirtya, Singaraja, Bali, Indonesia: c 1-3, z 1 (original drawings).
Library of the University, Leiden: h 1-6, i 1-7, j 1-8.
Museum voor Volkenkunde, Delft: d 3, d 4.
Rijks Museum voor Volkenkunde, Leiden: f 2, r 1, y 2.
I Gusti Ngurah Gdé Ngurah, Dyaksa Amlapura, Karang Asem, Bali, Indonesia: t 1.
Ida Wajan Raja, Boda Kling, Karang Asĕm, Bali, Indonesia: e 1 (original drawing).
I Ketut Bangbang Gdé Rawi (in his 'Sunar Agama'): r 2.
I Gusti Ngurah Ktut Sangka, Puri Agung, Krambitan, Tabanan, Bali, Indonesia: d 1, e 2-3, g 1-4, k 5, n 4, o 3, p 4, s 1-4, t 3-4.
School of Oriental and African Studies, University of London: y 1.
Institute for the Tropics: m 1, n 3.
Mrs. Drs. Alit Veldhuisen-Djajasoebrata, Museum voor Volkenkunde, Rotterdam: b 2.

BIBLIOGRAPHY

[1] ANGELINO, P. DE KAT, Balineesche Moedra's (handhoudingen der priesters), teekeningen door Tyra de Kleen, tekst van A. Adi-Poestaka, 's-Gravenhage, 1922.

[1] ANGELINO, P. DE KAT, Mudras auf Bali (Handhaltungen der Priester), Zeichnungen von Tyra de Kleen, Text von A. Folkwang Verlag, Hagen i. W. 1923.

[2] Bali, Studies in Life, Thought and Ritual, Van Hoeve, The Hague and Bandung, 1960.

[3] Bali, Further Studies in idem, W. van Hoeve Publishers Ltd., The Hague. 1969.

[4] BELO, JANE, Bali: Rangda and Barong, Monographs of the American Ethnological Society XVI, J. J. Augustin, New York, 1949.

[5] BELO, JANE, Bali: Temple Festival, MAES (as above), XXII same publisher, New York, 1953.

[6] BELO, JANE, Trance in Bali, Preface by Margaret Mead, Columbia University Press, New York, 1960.

[7] BELO, JANE, Traditional Balinese Culture, essays selected and edited by Jane Belo, Columbia University Press, New York—London, 1970.

[8] BOSCH, Dr. F. D. K., Een ontoelaatbaar experiment, Djawa 12, 1932, 258-59.

[9] BOSCH, Dr. F. D. K., Bali en de zending, Djawa 13, 1933, 1-39. Both papers reprinted.

[10] BOSCH, Dr. F. D. K., Selected studies in Indonesian Archaeology, The Hague, Nijhoff, '61.

[11] COOMARASWAMY, A. K. and Sister NIVEDITA, Myths of the Hindus and Buddhists, 1967.

[12] COVARRUBIAS, MIGUEL, Island of Bali, with an album of photographs by Rose Covarrubias, New York, Knopf, repeatedly reprinted.

[13] CRUCQ, K. C., Bijdrage tot de kennis van het Balisch doodenritueel, Ph. D. thesis Leiden, Mees, Santpoort, 1928.

[14] DRAKULIC, E. & others, Bali, Van Hoeve, The Hague, 1952.

[15] EERDE, J. C. VAN, Gebruiken bij den rijstbouw en rijstoogst op Lombok, Tijdschrift voor Indische Taal-, Land- en Volkenkunde 45, 1902, 563 sqq.

[16] FRIEDERICH, Dr. R., The civilization and culture of Bali, edited by Dr. R. Rost (or. ed. 1849), Susil Gupta Private Ltd., Calcutta-12, [1959].

[17] GONDA, Prof. Dr. J., Het Oud-Javaansche Brahmāṇḍa-Purāṇa, Proza-tekst en Kakawin, uitgegeven (Bibliotheca Javanica 5), vertaald (6), 1932 & 1933, Nix, Bandoeng.

[18] GORIS, Dr. R. (text) and Drs. P. L. DRONKERS (photography), BALI/Atlas Kebudajaan/Cults and Customs/Cultuurgeschiedenis in beeld. Pemerintah Republik Indonesia/Government of the Republic Indonesia/Regering van de Republiek Indonesia [1953].

[19] GOUDRIAAN, T. and HOOYKAAS, C., Stuti and Stava (Bauddha, Śiva and Vaiṣṇava) of Balinese brahman priests, Verhandelingen Koninklijke Nederlandsche Akademie van Wetenschappen, Afdeling Letterkunde, Nieuwe Reeks, 76, 1971, Amsterdam.

[20] HISS, PH. H., Bali, Duell, Sloan and Pierve, New York, 1941.

[21] HOOYKAAS, C., The lay of Jaya Prana, the Balinese Uriah, Luzac & Co., London, 1958.

[22] Idem, Agama Tirtha, Five Studies in Hindu-Balinese Religion, VKNAW (as above) 70/4, 1964.

[23] Idem, Surya-sevana, the way to God of a Balinese Siva priest, VKNAW 72/3, 1966.

[24] Idem, Balinese Bauddha Brahmans, VKNAW 77, 1973.

[25] Idem, Kama and Kala, materials for the study of Balinese shadow theatre, VKNAW, 1973.

[26] Idem, Cosmogony and creation in Balinese tradition, Bibliotheca Indonesica, Nijhoff, The Hague.

[27] HOOYKAAS-VAN LEEUWEN BOOMKAMP, Dr. JACOBA, Sprookjes en verhalen van Bali, Van Hoeve, 's-Gravenhage, Bandung, 1956.

[27] Idem, Märchen aus Bali, Die Waage, Zürich, 1963.

[28] Idem, Ritual Purification of a Balinese temple, VKNAW 68/4, Amsterdam 1961.

[29] Idem, De 'Goddelijke Gast' op Bali, I Bagoes Diarsa, Balisch gedicht en volksverhaal, Ph. D. thesis University of Indonesia, Bibliotheca Javanica 10, 1949.

[30] JUYNBOLL, Dr. H. H., Bali en Lombok, Catalogus van 's Rijks Ethnographisch Museum, VII, Brill, Leiden, 1912.

KAT ANGELINO, P. A. DE, cf. sub Angelino and Mudra.

[31] KATS, J., Sanghyang Kamahāyānikan, Oud-Javaansche tekst, Nijhoff, 's Gravenhage, 1910.

[32] KERSTEN, J., Bali, hoe een missionaris het ziet, De Pelgrim, Eindhoven, 1940.

KLEEN, TYRA DE (and P. de Kat Angelino), cf. Mudras.

[33] KRAEMER, Dr. H., De strijd over Bali en de zending, Paris, Amsterdam, 1933.

[34] LEKKERKERKER, C., Twee nieuwe werken over het Balische doodenritueel, Tijdschrift Nederlandsch Aardrijkskundig Genootschap, 1928, 906-12.

[35] MERSHON, K. E., Seven plus Seven, Mysterious life rituals in Bali, foreword by Margaret Mead, Vantage Press, Hollywood-New York, 1971.
[36] MOOJEN, P. A. J., Kunst op Bali, inleidende studie tot de Bouwkunst, Adi Poestaka, den Haag, 1926.
[37] MPU TANAKUNG, Śivarātrikalpa, an Old Javanese poem, its Indian source and Balinese illustrations, by A. Teeuw, Th. P. Galestin, S. O. Robson, P. J. Worsley and P. J. Zoetmulder, Bibliotheca Indonesica 3, The Hague, Martinus Nijhoff, 1969,
[38] Mudrās, the ritual hand-poses of the Buddha priests and the Shiva priests of Bali by Tyra de Kleen, with an introduction by A. J. D. Campbell, London-New York 1924.
[39] POERBATJARAKA, R. M. NG., Nītiçāstra, Oud-Javaansche tekst met vertaling, uitgegeven door, Bibliotheca Javanica 4, Nix, Bandoeng, 1933.
[40] POTT, Dr. P. H., Yoga and Yantra, The Hague, Nijhoff, 1966.
[41] PROOYE-SALOMONS, Dr. H. J. W. VAN, Gewijde verhalen en legenden van Hindoes en Boeddhisten, introd. Prof. Dr. W. Caland, Thieme, Zutphen.
[42] RAGHU VIRA, Prof. Dr., Sāra-samuccaya, a classical Indonesian compendium of high ideals, Śata-piṭaka Series 24, International Academy of Indian Culture, New Delhi 1962.
[43] SHARADA RANI, Ślokāntara, an Old Javanese didactic text, ib. 1957.
[44] SINGHAL, Mrs. Dr. SUDARSHANA DEVI, Gaṇapati-tattwa, an Old Javanese philosophic text, Śaṭa-piṭaka series, IAIC, New-Delhi, 1958.
[45] SOEBADIO, Dr. HARYATI, Jṇānasiddhānta, secret lore of the Balinese Śaiva-priest, Nijhoff, 's Gravenhage, 1971.
[46] SUDARSHANA DEVI, Wṛhaspati-tattwa, an Old Javanese philosophical text, Śaṭa-piṭaka Series, IAIC, New-Delhi, 1957. .
[47] SWELLENGREBEL, Dr. J. L., Een vorstenwijding op Bali, Mededelingen van het Rijks Museum voor Volkenkunde, Leiden, Brill, Leiden, 1947.
[48] Idem, Kerk en Tempel op Bali, Van Hoeve, 's Gravenhage, 1948.
[49] Idem, Studies in Life, thought and ritual [written by the best scholars, with a lengthy introduction by], Van Hoeve, The Hague and Bandung, 1960.
[50] WECK, WOLFGANG, Heilkunde und Volkstum auf Bali, Enke Verlag, Stuttgart, 1937.
[51] WIRZ, Dr. PAUL, Der Reisbau und die Reisbaukulte auf Bali und Lombok, Tijdschrift voor Indische Taal-, Land- en Volkenkunde, 67/3 & 4, 1927, 217-345.
[52] Idem, Der Totenkult auf Bali, mit 46 Figuren und 101 Abbildungen im Text und auf Tafeln, Strecker und Schroeder, Stuttgart, 1928.
[53] ZIESENISS, A., Studien zur Geschichte des Çivaismus, I, Die Çivaitischen Systeme in der Alt-Javanischen Literatur, Bijdragen tot de Taal-, Land- en Volkenkunde, uitgegeven door het Koninklijk Instituut voor de Taal-, Land- en Volkenkunde, 98/1 & 2, 1939, 75-223.
[54] Idem, II. Die Śaiva-Systematik des Vṛhaspati-tattva, International Academy of Indian Culture, New Delhi, 1958.
[55] ZOETE, BERYL DE, and WALTER SPIES, Dance and Drama in Bali, with a preface by Arthur Waley, Faber and Faber Ltd., London, 1938.
[56] ZOETMULDER, P. J., Old Javanese Literature, Nijhoff, 's Gravenhage, 1974.

De kunst van Bali, verleden en heden, Haags Gemeente-museum, The Hague, 1961.
Hedendaagse kunst van Bali, Centraal Museum, Utrecht, 1962.

Numbers between square brackets in the text refer to items in the bibliography in which more detailed information can be found.

1. Orientation

Bali is situated immediately to the east of Java with which it has strong cultural relation for more than a thousand years. Whereas Java since a few centuries must be reckoned to the world of Islam, Bali maintains its Hinduism which during several centuries it shared with Java. This Javano-Balinese culture will have been initiated by royal marriages but has certainly been consolidated by Javanese conquests of the island. Captains of the victorious army have been given grounds in most parts of the island; their present-day descendants are still very well aware of their Javanese ancestors. In many a case these feudal lords will have built a court and constituted groups for dance and drama. Scattered over the country nowadays about a hundred are still to be found. These barons had been courtiers of Majapahit and took with them the court literature, profane and theological, philosophic and ritualistic. From the cultural point of view, therefore, Bali is not only interesting in itself but perhaps even more so as a storehouse of Old-Javanese culture. It would be a mistake to consider Bali as a spiritual linear successor of Java, but its culture is partly pure Old-Javanese, for another part an adaptation of it.

(To the east of Bali, at a few miles' distance, is situated the island of Lombok. The Sasak language of this island is more similar with Balinese than is Javanese, structurally speaking, but then Balinese in course of time borrowed a not inconsiderable copia verborum from Javanese. During half of the eighteenth century and nearly entirely the nineteenth, princes of Bali ruled in (javanised, Muslim) Lombok, but this has not led to much cultural exchange in either direction).

Better to keep in mind that under the more or less Hinduised layer of the last ten centuries there is the common Indonesian base, pre-Christian, pre-Muslim and pre-Hindu. In this connection one should learn and never forget that Bali shares the word *tiwa(h)* with Kalimantan (Borneo of old), meaning the pomp of funeral ceremonies for a deceased person of royal rank [13, 52]. There exists a widely spread misunderstanding *re* cremation. The fire may be Hindu, but as a rule its purifying function is not invoked a few hours after death, as in Hindustan, but a few months, a few years after it, and in by far most cases never at all. There are better reasons for considering the Balinese to be Hindus, as may become clear in the course of this pamphlet. The good right of the Balinese to claim agama Hindu Bali, Balinese Hinduism, as their religion, will not be denied in these pages, but an endeavour is made to be fair to the different components of Balinese culture in general and of its religion in particular [16].

During the nineteenth century the northern fringe of Bali had some purely political contacts with the Netherlands' Indies' Government. In the first decade of this century the island lost its political independence. As early as twenty years later, for the first time, fear for loss of culture was felt by the Netherlands' Indies' Government. Allegedly palmleaf manuscripts were sold to tourists. To counteract this, a library of such mss., publicly accessible and much visited, was founded in the capital. Undoubtedly the loss of independence and the institution of a new kind of government must have shocked the population, and will have exercised a growing influence. The decade 1940-'50 will have shaken it considerably more [21]; to some extent the door to Indonesia had been opened but now it was opened to the world.

Those most accessible to Indonesian and European or American thought may be expected to become the leaders to the future and in the future and to become the most important people. When in an introductory pamphlet like this their minority does not yet find the room to which it might feel entitled already now or in a few decades' time, it is because this book in the main has to deal with traditional religion of the majority during the preceding ages [12].

2. First Acquaintance [18]

Using one's eyes in Bali one cannot fail to notice that every day crossroads are adorned with plaited offerings on the soil, invariably garnished with flowers or petals in bright colours. They are destined for the powers and forces of the netherworld; every layman and each of the six kinds of priests is conversant with the idea: *do ut abeas*, 'I give with the intention that thou mayest retire (and not harm us)'. This fundamental idea is demonstrated here and before the gates of dwellings, but then only on some definite days.

These crossroads, more often than not, are provided with awe-inspiring sculptures of demoniac beings (g 3, g 4), sometimes the goddess Durga. The leading thought again is their warding off of the spirits of evil. One should know that Kala, the God of Evil, at mid-day takes the crossroads as his hunting field.

Next fact that must strike anybody after having moved around only a few miles is the great number of temples [36]. One recognizes them immediately: whereas private courtyards are walled in to prevent eyes to roam over them, the two or three consecutive courts of a temple have lower walls with higher gates leading to higher buildings, some of them real pagodas and bearing the Indian name *méru*. These gates, called *chandi bĕntar*, 'split chandi', resembling a tall building lengthwise cut into two equal halves, immediately draws the attention due to their elaborate sculpture and their beautiful wooden doorwings. The fatal earthquake of 1917 destroyed or damaged seriously 2431 of Bali's temples on only one ninth of the island's surface, so that some >20.000 of them may exist, on a population then of about a million [2, 3]. This baffling number of an average of only fifty people available for the upkeep of a temple is the more serious because it originates from official figures and is given by Dr. R. Goris who makes a definite difference between a temple and a more humble common place of worship in the fields (a, b 1, k5). On top of that one should be aware that the stone used for the construction of any building is invariably of the easily accessible but extremely 'soft' quality that the island produces, *paras*. The task of the men is not unfrequently that of repairing damaged walls and buildings. The command of a village god, consulted because of an illness or disaster, through his medium in a state of trance, is only too often that those constructions should be renewed. Balinese religion asks a considerable amount of work from men and women.

The Balinese have no daily holy mass to attend and no weekly service, but their temples once in 210 days celebrate their anniversary [5]. Those temples are the places of worship for a local group, for members of a trade, for relatives of the same caste, but never for the god Siwa or the god Wisnu, as in India.

During that Balinese year of $5 \times 6 \times 7 = 210$ days several days are less favourable and will not have been chosen for the temple's anniversary so that a visitor, even when covering a considerable mileage, not necessarily somewhere stumbles upon such a celebration. But during the first part of the night he is bound to find musicians, actors and dancers practising for the coming temple festival; he cannot fail to see their petromax lamp and to hear their music and voices [55].

For such a temple festival an incredible amount of offerings has to be plaited, flowers collected, food prepared (m 3, o-q). Not unfrequently one sees a dozen of a village's women in an open building along the road busy with this job (o 1). It is not as heavy as that of the men but it takes many hours during several consecutive days. There may be much chatter and some coffee, true, but this temple business comes on top of the never ending daily offerings in the house, on the courtyard (k 5), in the domestic sanctuary, in the irrigated ricefields (a). It would be hazardous to say that the amount of time taken by religion in Bali is unprecedented, unrivalled, but there can be no doubt that the village population is kept busy with the practical and routine side of its religion [7].

This is a first impression and it remains true.

3. Kanda Mpat [26]

Not long after the Pacific War one could find mimeographed pamphlets on Balinese Hinduism, i.e. on how it should be believed and practised, written by Indians. Some of the members of staff of the Faculty of Arts, Udayana University of Denpasar, read in India for their academic exams and took their degrees there. BHAGAVAD-GITA, in English translation, and now even in Indonesian, is for sale in the Balinese bookshops. The Saraswati school organisation provides its students with lessons in religion. The Bureau for Religious Affairs last year was building a teachers' training college, consisting of several classrooms. The main subject to be read: religion, the future students meant to be specialists like their colleagues for geography or history. Whereas in the past temples were erected by groups who once in 210 days invited (mostly) local gods to descend to them from their aerial site above the top of the Great Mountain [5], recently a temple for the worship of Jagannath, Lord of the World, has been built. Hence the justified question: Are the XX. century and tourism changing everything in Bali? [32, 48].

For an adequate answer a depth of knowledge and a geographical and historical extent of experience is necessary, combined with a courage for prophesying which is nowhere to be found. But it is possible to deal with an example of an old belief which proves to be neither discarded nor doubted or intentionally ignored in the present. It should serve as an example, a to the world outside perhaps unexpected theme of belief that is quietly maintaining itself [50].

A Balinese dislikes being alone, either by day or by night. But then, he is not, for he is constantly accompanied by his four elder brothers when he is a male, four elder sisters in the case of a female (c 1, 2). They accompany him/her from shortly after conception till after cremation, actually till the final act of deliverance of the soul. They are the personified concomitants of his birth: the amniotic fluid, the blood, the vernix caseosa and the afterbirth. It is not well possible to preserve the first three, but the afterbirth is tangible enough. Shortly after birth it is buried outside the main-entrance to the sleeping house. A father leaving the door has it buried to the right in the case of a male child whereas the left side is given to the females. A river-stone of between ten to twenty kilogram covers this spot. Finally a fragment of the umbilical cord is preserved as an amulet, kept in a silver box, hung around the child's neck [35].

A sensible young mother, when giving the breast to her new-born baby, will not neglect first to spend a few drops of her milk to the floor, on behalf of the *kanda mpat*. She will continue doing so too when gradually passing from milk into rice by spilling a few grains of it in their honour. When the offerings of the rites de passage are presented on behalf of the small child, no careful parent or offering maker will forget to add those for its *kanda mpat*. At a tender age the child itself will learn to begin its meal only after spilling a very little bit to his omnipresent companions. In a manual for a Buddhist brahman priest we find the exhortation not to go to sleep before having spent some friendly thoughts upon the *kanda mpat* [24]. This is only a wise precaution, for in the case of being neglected they might turn nasty. When the officiating priest has reached a critical stage in his daily worship because now he is about to expel all evil beings, his manual recommends him to be aware of the existence of his four elder brothers. Their physiognomy, when depicted in the treatises dealing with them, is rather impish, and the place where offerings are given to them is shared with evil *bhuta* and *kala*. One never sees them, unless as a result of black magic, but in danger is reconforted by feeling their helpful presence.

When in the late 'thirties final care for the dead (*maligia*) was bestowed upon since long cremated persons belonging to the court of Karang Asĕm, to the existing turrets for their ashes (*bukur*) one was added for their *kanda mpat* [35].

Nobody is ignorant about their names, Anggapati, Mrajapati, Banaspati and Banaspati-Raja (c 1, c 2). Most people moreover will know that the *kanda mpat* are also known by other names, to begin during the foetal development of the baby, but not everybody knows by heart all those sets of four in which the treatises take delight. Characteristic for Balinese thinking is that they are identified with sages from the hoary past, with the rebellious sons of the Supreme God, who were changed into ungainly animals and banished to the four directions. They began to feel repentant, however (c 3), and then became the gods Iswara, Brahma, Mahadewa and Wisnu. When hearing about this the little child, himself *bhuwana alit*, 'small world, microcosm', at an early age learns to feel himself as being part of *bhuwana agung*, 'large world, macrocosm', and to behave himself accordingln. This feeling ot relationship between *bhuwana agung* and *bhuwana alit* is not only modery but ancient: in the old Hindu-Balinese mysticism reference is made to the *sat-kahyangan ing raga*, the six divine centres in the human body, whereas the usual *sat-kahyangan* are six famous sanctuaries in Bali (different according to the province in which one lives) [49].

In the small publications during the last years emanating from Bureaus for Religious Affairs and from other sides the *kanda mpat* are recommended in the readers' attention [26].

4. Some Dangers

We are used to find in a country of the Western sphere that shortly after harvesting time provincial authorities keep a thanksgiving day. The Balinese, certainly not less keen on having a good harvest [51], for all of them a serious matter, annually take steps to promote their harvest by trying to forestall disasters or at least to minimise them [15]. To that purpose in Gianiar and Klungkung rituals of *nangluk marana* are held; perhaps elsewhere as well. *Marana* is Sanskrit and means 'death', *nangluk* is Balinese and means 'exclusion'. Officiating priests are the fourth caste *pamangku*, village- or temple-priest (k), as well as the brahman priest of the first caste, the *padanda* (m), whose ritual is rich in Sanskrit [1]. Government is represented by its highest functionaries down to the lower ranks, for the ritual is held on behalf of the whole province. According to popular belief the devastating mice take their origin from fishes, approaching from the island Nusa Pěnida to the south-east. Therefore the ceremonies are held at the shore.

The date for the yearly celebration of *nangluk marana* is chosen in such a way that the season helps to diminish the plague. If, however, the calamity continues, another stratagem is adopted: each house-father has to contribute one mouse, and they are cremated in their thousands, following the same ritual as is practised for human beings. The basic idea must be that after this ritual malevolent spirits have been pacified and no longer feel attracted to harrass mankind. This procedure is reputed to work much better than poison.

It is only too evident in an agricultural community, moreover living under the refined circumstances of having irrigated fields to a considerable extent, that a sufficient amount of water is indispensable and that drought is a danger. As the idea of vow and propitiating the deities has its natural course in Bali and Lombok, Government periodically sent a brahman priest to the most important lakes of Bali and Lombok to invoke the benevolence of their goddesses. In order to promote this state of mind small golden replicas of aquatic animals were offered to her. To that purpose the priest makes the climb from the hot plains to the cold shore of the lake. Shivering in his white ritual cloth, not made for these circumstances, he conducts his service and throws the gold into the lake.

Another means of acquiring the goddess' benevolence is to offer a waterbuffalo to her. It is drowned in the lake. Many village temples have their unroofed seat for the worship of the god of the High Mountain flanked by one for the Goddess of the Lake.

ASTUPUNGKU [25] is the name of a long and complicated *mantra* destined to counteract all kinds of dangers. It is certainly old, and as it is known to all priests distinguished by a sufficient training of the memory, we may expect that the most numerous but less trained category, that of the *pamangku*, will use parts of it. It consists of nine sections of unequal length, assumedly of independent origin, but spoken always in the same sequence and expected to be useful under all circumstances. As the composition into a ninefold formula may have taken place in a brahman *griya*, where everybody is conversant with litanies directed towards the four directions, the four between them and the centre, this *navaratna*, 'ninefold jewel', may participate in the same trend of thought.

1. Deals with the numerous dangers to which are exposed those born in a certain week.
2. Enumerates the fifteen cases in which the composition of the family is ominous.
3. Consists of threats emanating from fire, water, lightning, but also Durga, Earth, the Guardians of the Directions and Guru Paduka, the Supreme God Teacher.
4. Enumerates the 30 names of the seven-day week; the meaning must be to remind that each of them has its ominous days according to *wariga*, astrological table.
5. Here one is 'the victim of' numerous mishaps. It begins with a seemingly harmless thing: 'when a small houselizard falls on thee', but it ends with the calamity of the collapsing of a rice granary.
6. Consists of an enumeration of configurations of the ground and of special spots from which emanate lethal influences which, after consulting a geomancer should be avoided (z).

7. Enumerates the mortal danger arising from curses, treachery, stratagems, temptations, seduction, evil words and evil deeds, hidden power and prohibitions.
8. Deals with dangers emanating from the acts of evildoers, from their poison and sorcery.
9. Gives a long enumeration, sometimes making the impression of having been a metrical litany, of all bodily deformities and the incurable illnesses to which those people are subject whose souls proceed from Yamani-loka, Hell.

Apparently mankind is threatened by many dangers (hi); the various priests know how to counteract them (j).

Swearing an oath may be concluded with the words: "may God Almighty help me". In Bali the invocation of celestial beings as witnesses was followed by a curse having the tenor: "if I break this oath, may I be annihilated by this or that power". One of these powers consists of the Pancha-Rĕsi, cf. Kanda Mpat.

In this connection it is worthwhile to point to the existence of a grotto of bats along the metalled road between Klungkung and Karang Asem, the temple in front of it and the oath sworn there in the beginning of this century by two Regents of Bali. This awe-inspiring place lodged more than flapping of wings, shrill cries and stench. There is an inherent danger here, and the passing coach stops for a moment to deposit an offering, mutter a mantra and placate the spirit.

5. Impurity

It is only evident that an agricultural community, moreover working in the tropics, often feels unclean, dirty. The mountainous landscape and the favourable climate of Bali everywhere open the possibility of daily complete cleansing of the body, pleasantly together in the open air. Hand in hand with the material cleansing goes a strong need for spiritual purification, while using the material terminology. *Toya*, water, has the special meaning of Holy Water, of which a dozen different kinds is known. *Dus* and *dyus* are words for taking a bath, but *padudusan*, lustration, is a so frequent ritual that a minor and a major administration of it are practised. The representative of a village, of a province and even the governor of the island may be the subject of such a lustration. Then first a cock picks away the defilements from his breast, next a drake (d 2) and finally a male piglet.

The Sanskrit word *suchi* means 'light' and 'bright' in the usual, material sense of the word as well as 'holy, virtuous, honest' in the spiritual sense. In Indonesian *chuchi* is only used in the material field; in Bali it does not mean that one is 'virtuous' or 'holy' but that he has undergone an initiation.

For 'impurity' the Sanskrit word *mala* has been borrowed and in innumerable *mantra* one comes across *tri-mala, pañcha-mala, daśa-mala,* being three-, five- and tenfold impurity, from which purification is requested. The decad runs as follows: 1. touched by an unclean being; 2. besmirched by toilet-powder; 3. when a hair has fallen on thee; 4. when a cockerel flies over thee; 5. when a dog steps over thy body; 6. when chafed by meat or fish; 7. when ... has fallen on thee; 8. after a purchase on the market; 9. when robbed in a gambling den; 10. when a small child (soils?) thee.

A menstruating woman should not receive a guest or enter a temple, being unclean. After having given birth a young mother is considered as being ritually unclean; only after a ritual by water and by fire on the 35 + 7th day she is readmitted as normal in society.

When a lady of high caste gave birth to twins of different sex, this was considered as being meritorious and an advantage for her village, for the babies on this elevated level of society were destined to be a couple (cf. the pharaohs of Egypt). When, however, a commoner gives birth to twins of different sex, this act of presumption and the babies' supposed incest in the womb were considered to defile the house (which had to be burned down) and the village (which had to be left by the unfortunate family, for the next 42 days to be transferred to a shed on the graveyard) [7].

This idea of a whole community being defiled by impurity is common. A temple will be closed for some time because its *pĕmangku* has found that something untoward has befallen it. Even a whole province can decide that it feels soiled and unclean, that it needs to be freed from its impurity. Then the gods of the most representative temple are taken to the sea to be purified ritually. This is not a matter of some temple priests only, but of hundreds if not even thousands of followers as well. They and the keepers of stalls along the road who quench their thirst and still their hunger, and those who help them to find some rest during the night, at reduced prices or even for the sake of the ceremony, pleasing to the gods—they all are acting in the firm belief that they are helping to remove impurity. Here it is water which works purification; of old, when a country had to be purified, a fire offering called *homa* was brought (last time in Lombok, 1933). One recognizes the two elements of purification, also at the occasion of a cremation: water and fire.

A provincial ceremony as sketched above, *pancha-bali-krama*, 'fivefold offering ritual', can be held every five years, but only once in a century (or once in a life's time) on behalf of the whole island an enormous purificatory ritual is held in the state sanctuary of Besakih, on the slope of the highest mountain, the Gunung Agung. This huge ceremony, in which the governor of the island is the subject of the *padudusan*, is called Eka-daśa-Rudra. Rudra is the most terrific aspect of the uppergod Siwa; *éka-daśa* means eleven, that is the four directions, the four between them, nadir, zenith and centre. Such a cosmic event has to be prepared and helped in advance, so that during the months of preparation as many as possible human remains, buried provisionally in the vague hope that some time the necessary and considerable means for a decent cremation will be found, now are given a cremation.

Dyus, *dudus* and *padudusan*, words for bathing, often interchange with *lukat* and *panglukatan* (d 2, d 3). The *padanda*, brahman priest, every morning as the result of his worship of Siwa the God of the Sun, or of Buddha, prepares *toya pabrĕsihan*, Holy water for purification (reckoned from reasonable purity upwards) and *toya panglukatan*, Holy Water provided with exorcising qualities (empowered to rub off existing but intolerable impurities [22; 24]. His cousins, brahmans like him, but not (yet) consecrated to full priesthood (to the state of "high priest" as several books on Bali have it) who have preferred to be performers of the shadow theatre and are entitled to being called *amangku dalang*, prepare such Holy Water by dipping the handles of a chosen set of *ringgit*, puppets, into clean water, accompanied by *mantra* and *mudra*, gestures of the fingers (n). The impurity to be washed away with this kind of water may be that of the living as well as that of the dead. It may be of (hoped) temporary nature, as when a child is intractable, or permanent, as when a child is born on the wrong day or in a wrong composition of the family (for instance five brothers, which is presumptuous, since mythology knows the five Pandawa brethren) [25].

Much could have been extended and added, but at this stage the reader should only be pervaded by the ordinary Balinese feeling of frequent, accidental, external and rather material impurity, which, however, makes him feel unhappy and desirous of help and of Holy Water.

6. Demons

The *kanda mpat* are not a mere ornament in the life of a Balinese for he is constantly harrassed by hords and armies of malevolent beings of the most divergent shape, function, abode and time of activity—one would nearly say: as many as a playful mind during many hours of leisure can imagine. When the exorcist priest, the *sĕngguhu* or *rĕsi bhujangga* during an important ritual recites his long litany PURWA BHUMI TUWA/KAMULAN, when he has had a good teacher and himself has a good memory, he enumerates tens, dozens, scores of names and locates them everywhere in our immediate neighbourhood. He belongs to the fourth caste and invokes and pacifies a set of demons entirely different from those which the brahman priest handles during rites of exorcism. He has to convoke them, to regale them and finally to invite them to go home to their respective quarters at a safe distance in the four directions. They are of course much feared, not only by little children, so that it makes such a good-humoured effect when the officiating priest in his long *mantra* of sending home the *bhuta* and *kala* tells them: "Now here (on the ground) are the offerings destined for thee. When it is not yet enough I offer thee some cash; take it to the great market and there buy what thy needest. After that kindly go home, without fail each to his own quarters".

Whereas those administered by the exorcist priest are only distinguished by name and location, those pacified by the *padanda,* at least during death ritual, can have something to do with ethics. The priest uses the Sanskrit word *dosa,* sins, and these are distinguished in insignificant, usual and colossal ones, the expiation (*panĕbusan*) for which consists of offerings on the same scale. The making of these time-devouring offerings comes to rest upon the shoulders of the relatives, but the expenses are taken from the heritage before splitting it up on behalf of the heirs. So to some extent the dead man has to pay for his sins and the word 'expiation' must be taken in this sense.

One should avoid crossroads at mid-day, for Kala, the frightful Lord of Demons, then and there looks for his prey. One should not leave his house during the night without singing, or after having quarelled. This is the time when beings consisting of a mere head, or of a thigh with a devouring mouth, are roaming everywhere, but especially at crossroads and above all in the graveyard (h). As long as the dead have not yet been cremated and thus purified by the Fire of God and the various Holy Water prepared by the *padanda,* temporary seat of God, their unpacified spirits roam about and might be harmful—and everybody has some such relatives in the greater family.

Perhaps feared most of all are the *léyak* who may wound and even kill human beings. *Bhuta* and *kala* come from the outside and may go away again, but *léyak* are amongst us with their sorcery. They are worse, just like civil war is worse than war with a foreign enemy.

Fortunately there are several means to deceive and to deter the Powers of Evil (h 5, h 6).

To forestall their entry to private courtyards, immediately after the gate a solid stone screen forces us to go to the left or to the right, but the rectilinear evil beings either crash or return. Kala, the incorporation of Evil, spying upon one and the other, may find them under the protection of a *mangku dalang*. And then without exception the Lord of *bhutas* and *kalas* is outwitted by this priest who cheats him, who is able to read the *mantra* written on Kala's body, who himself knows his *mantra* from his writing DHARMA PAWAYANGAN [25].

In his constant battle against all the invisible malevolent beings the Balinese is helped by his different kinds of priests, half a dozen of them at least. They are padanda Siwa and padanda Buddha (m), the *ulaka* who has not yet received his final consecration but to some extent deputises for the padanda. There is the *amangku dalang* (n), as a rule a brahman like him, who has received his performer's consecration. There are the *balians* or witch doctors, the few *dukuhs*, mainly in Karang Asem, and the *sengguhus* and *rĕsi bhujangga* in the other provinces. Divine beings appear to be necessarily followed by a less holy retinue, and that may be the reason why the *pamangku*, temple priest (k), in their thousands, also help to conjure down *bhuta* and *kala*, but their stronger side lies in the worship of the gods.

The heading 'demons' may be too outspoken, but here is the least inappropriate place to relate that those living in the southeast of Bali are convinced that periodically inimical powers invade from the sea. They may come swimming like fishes in their numbers and harrass the agriculturists in the shape of mice, or they choose to be germs of maladies of mankind. During such a period of fear no courtyard will fail to hang up its menacing signs to chase them off.

7. Black Magic

Many Balinese are convinced that they can be made the victims of black magic, and judging from the not-unfrequent occurrence of manuals on magic, called KAWISESAN, the number of those who exercise it should not be underrated. Formulas and drawings are the most frequent means, *srana*, but several more are mentioned in the treatises. For instance; "Take a nutmeg, write (or: draw) Yama-Raja on it, and the name of the person you aim at, put it in your house-shrine, cover it up with rice-chaff, let it smoulder, as long as seven days and seven nights". Yama-Raja is the Judge in the Hereafter and thus the inescapable Lord of Punition [22].

Another example: "When you aim at confounding your enemy: write (or draw) Yama-Raja on a strip of palmleaf, burn it to ashes and mix them with ricegrains; scatter them on the road; first draw a thunderbolt on the road." We already learned that the man who wished to see his *kanda mpat* had to submit himself to conditions which were (next to) impossible to fulfill; this is not an exception.

At the celebration of the Eka-daśa-Rudra [24] a more or less cubic, in any case rectangular piece of masonry is made with a drawing of Yama-Raja on it. This is the supreme ritual at which the *stutis* in honour of Yama-Raja are recited by the senior padanda Buddha, the only one to know them and to use them in his ritual. But when we see a sculpture of Yama-Raja in the *puri*, baronial court of Kaba-kaba, there is no question of Buddhism but here we have to do with the Yama-Raja of all Balinese (e). His front consists of three times three squares inscribed with syllables, just like a drawing of Yama-

Raja is provided with five times five syllables. They are the materials used to read the magic formulas in the form of Indian *anustubh,* four lines of eight syllables, devised to destroy the enemy and safeguard the self [22].

The application of such a Sanskrit formula may be disastrous, but those gifted with self-confidence and provided with a knowledgeable priest may counteract such a curse with *balik sumpah,* reversal of curse, of which numerous collections have come down to us, justifying the conviction that at least in the recent past the Balinese were prone to curses and counter-curses.

8. Holy Water(s)

When in § 5 impurity was dealt with, cleansing, water and Holy Water were also mentioned. This matter has only been broached with the mention of *toya pabrĕsihan* and *toya panglukatan.* The head of the Bureau for Religious Affairs in West-Lombok, Hinduist and Buddhist, once kindly showed me three ponds in the immediate neighbourhood of the former royal park Sura-nadi, 'River of the Gods'. The ponds were called *toya pabrĕsihan, toya panglukatan,* and the third *toya pangĕntas.* This means: 'water having the capacity to ship over (sc. the soul) from the undesired side of the water to the other side'. During the ritual for the dead it is prepared and applied after many ritual acts as the final and decisive one before the dead body (or its substitute) is put in its vehicle (according to caste, social position and wealth) and conducted to the graveyard where the flames will add their purifying power to that of the waters. These ponds, I scarcely need to say, represent a playful side of Balinese belief, which did neither prevent this public servant to show them to me, nor the Hindu and Muslim inhabitants of the neighbourhood to build there several bathing sheds and to feel the profit from their baths.

Toya pangĕntas is certainly from the highest importance for the Balinese in their care of the dead, but an enumeration of the different kinds of Holy Water has not come to an end with it. These were the three which the *padanda* prepares at the cost of much time with a considerable amount of ritualistic skill. The last, however, of several Holy Waters to be poured on a dead body about to be cremated, *kakuluh,* is not prepared by him but by the *pamangku,* and not as the result of the muttering of numerous *mantra* and the making of many *mudra,* but by simply putting a bowl with pure water on the unroofed seat destined for Siwa God of the Sun in (one of) the village temples, accompanied by a short prayer expressing the hope that during the night He may deign to descend into the water and in doing so making it partake in His Divinity.

Preceding water in the ritual for the dead is the *toya pamanahan,* Holy Water obtained by the priest's shooting an arrow into it, an activity considered to be cosmic to such a degree that the Pancha-rĕsi, the Five Seers in the Sky, are considered to partake in it. The *padanda* may make this in public as well as in the solitude of his own domestic sanctuary, *pamrajan* (called after his most potent cult instrument, the *wajra,* the thunderbolt). His manuals tell him, however, to prepare *toya panyĕhĕb* in the solitude of his *pamrajan,* during the night. This toya should not be *sprinkled on* the dead body but it should be *thrown lengthwise over* it.

None of these waters is the result of anything else than one priest's prayers when squatting in self-concentration on one place. Other brands, to know *tirtha kamandalu, tirtha sanjivani, tirtha kundalini* and *tirtha maha-mĕrta,* needed during death ritual and as to their origin located at the four sides of the Méru, the Mountain of the World, are likewise prepared by the *padanda* while squatting in lotus position. But I remember vividly how during a very rainy celebration of the temple anniversary of Champuan, Ubud (Gianiar), soaking messengers, wet to the bone, returned from their rainy mission to the Great Mountain where they had fetched water considered to be more pure and effective than any from the sources in the neighbourhood.

This was not the only pure water serving as basic material to be transsubstantiated into Holy Water; much had to be fetched from the *beji*, a well of water considered to be sufficiantly pure. A *pamangku*, on this important mission honoured by a cortege of well-clad and weaponed (blowing pipe) people, takes care of the necessary prayers and offerings to the *beji*. Such a cortege is frequent, gay and beloved. Eventually the young son of him who pays for the whole ceremony may be put on a palanquin and in this honoured position draw much attention, or a score of young girls in full apparel march faultlessly one after the other, the smalles in front, the tallest at the rear.

The Balinese certainly thoroughly enjoy these occasions, and the activities of the *pamangku*, asking for pure water, makes that nobody forgets that this pure water is the main thing. The water does not cost a cent but is the only thing asked for ritually. The animals to be slaughtered during the diverse ceremonies (p 1) and the rice to be steamed, to feed sometimes hundreds and even thousands of people, are only patiently collected during the months and during the years, but the pure water to become Holy Water is asked for and fetched in a festive cortege.

When during one of Bali's yearly 20.000 temple festivals a *padanda* is invited to prepare the necessary Holy Water, during this preparation the worshippers mill around him as during any popular festival, not paying the slightest heed to him who is engaged on conducting the soul of the Supreme God Siwa to his own body. No business of theirs. Only when they are made aware that the Holy Water has been prepared, they become silent to the last man. They witness how It is offered to the seat of Siwa and then receive their own share, to their external and internal well-being. It gives a feeling of unity with God, of regained purity and strengthened physical and psychical powers. The Balinese were in the habit of calling their religion, *agama*, the *agama tirtha*, the religion of Holy Water [28].

9. Priests: Pamangku [5]

When the number of temples is put at some 20.000 and all of them employ a temple priest, *pamangku*, their number is enormous. In fact it might be the multiple of the other priests taken together (k).

His most humble role consists of his keeping clean the temple with its two or three rectangular courts, spacious enough to contain the shrines of the gods, the buildings of utility and the worshippers during the temple's anniversary. He must, moreover, pay heed to the upkeep of buildings and enclosing walls. When he didn't he would risk that during the periodical temple festival the goddess of the temple might make known through the voice of a medium in trance that mishaps in the village should be explained by this negligence.

During the days of celebration of the temple's anniversary, once in 210 days, he and his wife are extremely busy because all the families of worshippers supporting this sanctuary bring their offerings to the gods and need his help for the uttering of the correct formula or the proper alignment. It is the *pamangku* who conducts the service: he invites the temple-gods to descend from their lofty abodes above the Great Mountain and temporarily to take their abode in their private shrines, the greater gods to deign to settle in the communal building destined for them. He invites them to go to the *béji*, source, to refresh themselves by taking a bath. Having conducted them back he provides them with the offerings destined for them. These offerings with their various colours and shape are not only a pleasure to the eye, but as the various fruits have been fastened on thin sticks, the juice spreads a delicious fragrance. During the night the gods enjoy the opportunity of eating the *sari*, essence; next day the housewives who made these offerings take the material leavings home and consume them with their family.

On top of fruits and cakes the treat of the gods consists of the music of the percussion instruments, the *gong*, and dramatic performances, human actors and dancers, using or not using masks, or a performance of the shadow theatre. Remarkably enough, during the celebration of such an anniversary as well as at the consecration of a building, *pamlaspas*, the pamangku's manuals declare that the gods like to hear the recitation of the poem WARGASARI. It is done in a way which must be very traditional and old-fashioned, showing much likelihood with braying or lowing; the performer, an aged man, keeps a hand before his mouth.

The pamangku may help his villagers to kakuluh, prepared by himself, and to *tirtha*, prepared by the *padanda*. The *padanda* maintains his squatting position, the *pamangku* and his wife are moving around while administering *tirtha*. This distribution of Holy Water is not the only field of cooperation between *padanda* and *pamangku*. Time and again *padandas* of both denominations felt called upon to write a manual for the *pamangku*. In 1958 the Central bureau for Religious Affairs in the capital Denpasar published a mimeographed Buddhist version in which homage was paid to Buddha, Dharma (Law, Ethics) and Sanggha (the community of believers). Not long after I found it in a distant village in Gianiar, in the usual way grooved in prepared leaves of the palmtree. In 1972 the Bureau for Religious Affairs in the province Tabanan had the usual (Saiwa) version republished. According to the manuscripts of the *pamangkus* themselves they should have received their ritual from Mpu Kuturan, brother to Mpu Bharadah, the brahman renovator of religion in the hoary past. It is not yet possible to determine whether the *pamangkus* have borrowed part of their ritual from the *padandas* like the *rĕsis bhujangga* have done (cf. 12) but it is a fact beyond doubt that numerous litanies used by them have the *griya* as their origin. And of course a not inconsiderable number of Sanskrit words and *mantra*.

The manual for the *pamangku*'s ritual, the GAGELARAN PAMANGKU, has the subtitle KUSUMA-DEWA. These words, meaning 'The God of Flowers', i.e. Kama, not appearing as appropriate for the *pamangku*, could have been expected for the *amangku dalang*, who in his ritual several times claims to be the God Kama. But then, proper research on Bali's different priests, their spheres of activities and their past has scarcely begun.

Apart from the upkeep of the temple and the celebration of its anniversary the *pamangku* helps his villagers with the formulation of vows and the offering to be made when a vow has been answered. Vows are frequent and can be most picturesque, as when people, not used to horse-riding, once a year are mounted.

We saw the *pamangku* as the main priest; frequently, moreover, he is indispensable as a helper, or he may deputise. At *Nyĕpi*, when offerings should be brought at all crossroads, often he takes the place of the *sĕngguhu*, of whom there simply aren't enough. He assists at a burial, but for a cremation the *padanda* try to monopolise. However, a *pamangku* enjoying the repute of giving efficacious medicine, of being able to detect lost or stolen possessions, of knowing 'sharp' *mantras*, will succeed in the fields of other priests as well, especially when they are not within easy reach; the boundaries are not always well-marked.

When a celebration is important and the feasters arrive in their hundreds and thousands, as many as ten or even twenty *pamangkus* help one another.

10. Priests: Padanda (m)

In insular Southeast Asia it is traditional to indicate an elevated person by chiselling his feet in the rock or by speaking about him and addressing him with: 'the feet' or 'covering of the feet'. In Bali *Chokor-da* is the highest feudal title, *pada-n-da* is used for the brahman or 'high' priest; both are words for 'foot'. The *padanda* is far from illiterate for it takes him years to learn the various rituals. First of all he has to be experienced in the daily adoration of Siwa Aditya or Siwa Surya, Siwa in His aspect as the God of the Sun. This *Surya-sewana*, worship of the Sun, a ritual which takes about an hour in the early morning, results in the preparation of two kinds of *tirtha*. It is preceded by the priest's circumstantial cleansing himself materially; it goes on with his burning away of his last defilements, so that the soul of Siwa deigns descend into him. In this way it is possible to prepare these waters [23].

They are the base of any other ritual, for instance when the *padanda* is invited to officiate in *bhuta-yajña*, offering to the *bhuta* and *kala*, in order to get rid of them. He also takes care of *manusa-yajña*, offering to mankind, i.e. the rites de passage meant to undo the dangers menacing the foetus, the baby, the child, the puber and the bride and groom. He is responsable for *pitra-yajña*, the offerings which must bring the soul of the deceased to their state of deity in heaven, or to final liberation. Considering the first-mentioned ritual, *surya-sewana*, as *déwa-yajña*, and leaving controversial *rĕsi-yajña* out of the picture, we have to do with an official five-fold task of the *padanda* [24].

These five fields, frequently repeated in numerous mimeographed and printed pamphlets, certainly give a general idea, but they are still far from exhaustive. Often the help of the *padanda* is invoked for *mlaspas*, inauguration, of a building, *balé*, of a *sanggah*, altar, and of a *padmasana*, 'lotus-seat', to which Siwa Aditya is invited to descend.

Just like before a cremation the soil in the graveyard has to be purified, so the ground destined for a building will be made the subject for a ritual of purification. Elaborate ritual is needed for the purification of a temple.

In the past a candidate for *padanda*-ship may have served his teacher and his wife in their compound in the Indian way as described in the ADI-PARWA. But nowadays he has to make himself accepted first by a *padanda* who teaches him the subject (which he has to memorise in his own home) and finally by another who gives him the consecration. This ceremony is very impressive; the candidate at a certain stage is considered and dealt with as if he were a corpse and then is resuscitated to new life; he is reborn—the same thought as with the consecration of a new Roman-Catholic priest. He gets his initiator's foot on his head and is allowed to kiss its great toe. At the same time the new *padanda*'s wife of equal birth undergoes the ceremony; she is his help, his deputy and perhaps his successor [2]. Even unmarried and divorced brahman priestesses are known.

During his ritual the *padanda* squats in one place, even if it lasts for hours at a stretch. This is part of his *yoga*, exertion, and he is very well aware of *dhyana/samadhi*, concentration of thinking, and of *pranayama*, breath-control. Frequently he must be assisted for practical things; as his wife is not always able or willing to do so, he is served by an *ulaka* (from *walaka*, *balaka*, child, junior). To this assistant number of activities and even rituals are confided. There are no written rules how far this may go and much will depend on the age and the health of the *padanda* who has been invited to ... *muput karya*, i.e. to finish or complete a ritual. This choice of words illustrates that the deputising by a not yet ordained priest is felt as being: by a junior priest. A newly ordained *padanda* may be invited for the pacifying of *bhuta* and *kala*, followed by their chasing them home, but a few years must have elapsed before the most important task is confided to him; the care of the dead. And even so he may fail in the difficult task of 'shipping over to the right side' the soul of the deceased, so that it haunts the sleep of the bereaved ones. Then it may err along the waters and frequent the crossroads, so that there sometimes one can see a priest at work, trying to conduct it yet to its destination.

Surya means sun; as the padanda Siwa during his worship purifies and empties himself to offer an abode for Siwa the God of the Sun, it is only natural when the layman, speaking about the *padanda*, whose wife he asks for *toya*, calls the reverend man 'my Surya'. Likewise when the *padanda* happens to follow the Buddha ritual, he remains 'my Surya', for the *sisya*, the layman, is not interested in their entirely different methods of preparation of Holy Water. The *sisya* is not so pernickety; moreover, how could he be?

11. PRIESTS: AMANGKU DALANG [25]

Anybody in Balinese society is allowed to establish himself as a *dalang*, puppeteer of the shadow-theatre. Such a nightly performance can be arranged for purely secular and mercenary purposes. Frequently, however, it is given at the occasion of rites de passage, specially marriage. Then the choice of the play is not arbitrary but appropriate to the occasion.

Whereas the ordinary *dalang* performs during the night, uses screen and lamp, needs hours after hours for a more or less secular performance, the *amangku dalang* uses neither lamp nor screen, only a thread supporting the *ringgits* leaning to it, a thread tended between two branches of the ever-sprouting magically important *dapdap* tree (n). His performance, frequently at mid-day, at the same time as that of a *sĕngguhu*, lasts for about one hour only and at the best attracts some stray children as the visible part of his auditory. His aim is religious, exorcistic; often it is a child which is the object of his *lukat*, but not necessarily so. The child may be intractable, have been born on the wrong day or in the wrong composition of family.

The performance with the *ringgits* certainly exercises its healthy influence but above all the *amangku dalang* is expected to exorcise by the force of the Holy Water, *toya panglukatan*, which he prepares after the performance by sticking handles of certain puppets into holy water, accompanied by the muttering of the appropriate *mantras* and the making of the necessary *mudras*. The *amangku dalang* should know by heart several scores of shorter and longer *mantras* which he learns from the DHARMA PAWAYANGAN, 'thesaurus of *mantras* fit for the shadowplay'. They are conceived in that kind of Sanskrit, deprived of declension and conjugation, doing only with a very few verbs, called 'Archipelago-Sanskrit', which is also found in many *mantras* used by the *padandas*.

It would be misleading to suggest that *toya panglukatan*, prepared by the *amangku dalang*, were only needed for children. Grown-ups may as well need it badly during several of the most different unfortunate situations in life. Its beneficial working is not restricted to the living, under certain circumstances the dead are as well helped by it.

12. Priests: Sengguhu

For two reasons the *sĕngguhu*, from the half dozen of Balinese priests, deserves to be dealt with in relation with the brahman *amangku dalang*. First because he is also an exorcist (but without any side of entertainment), secondly because at major occasions he begins his ritual by making Holy Water exactly like his one teacher, the *padanda*. From his *sĕngguhu* teacher he learns another section of his mantraic apparel and above all the litany PURWA BHUMI, 'cosmogony', followed either by TUWA, 'old', or by KAMULAN, 'origin(al)'. When officiating under these circumstances he is robed and mitred as a *padanda* and claims the title *rĕsi bhujangga*. *Rĕsi* denotes a seer in India's far past; *pancha-rĕsi* and *sapta-rĕsi* are a pentad and a septad of them, elevated to heavenly rank and known to literate Indians and Balinese. But *rĕsi* in Bali has the special meaning of 'person not belonging to the rank of a brahman but mastering his daily ritual'. In the case of those belonging to the intermarrying group of the *sĕngguhu*, officially ranked as being *sudra* or *jaba* ('outside', i.e. outside the three higher Hindu castes, *tri wangsa*), this is conform reality, for he is instructed in the complete *surya-séwana*. But when a *ksatrya*, belonging to the second caste, that of the 'warriors' or military men, wishes to learn to prepare his own Holy Water and thus become a *rĕsi*, in the main two differences can be noted. First the *mantras* directed to Siwa are augmented with a final word being one of Wisnu's names, so that the nobleman is worshipping Wisnu. Secondly the essential element in *Surya-séwana*, consisting of the divine descent of Siwa into the worshipper, is skipped—perhaps because he is worshipping Wisnu.

Once a year an energetic endeavour is made to chase all demons from the island and to make them believe that it is deserted, *sĕpi*, and not worthwhile ever to return to again. This observation of the state of *nyĕpi*, consisting of minimalising traffic and forbidding to have smoke from cooking fires as well as from sigarettes, is preceded by the *sĕngguhu*'s chasing off the *bhutas* and *kalas*. To that purpose he chooses a village's main crossroads as his field of action; while he drones the recital of his litany by the uninterrupted ringing of his bell, his helpers add considerably to the noise by eliciting the full power from a small handdrum and from a disc to which five bells are attached.

The lighting of fire under pieces of still green bamboo aims at the sound of explosions. All over the world noise has a deterrant effect; the averting of (more) disaster can be effectuated by adding the maximum of noise to be caused by a complete *gong* to the din already made by the *sĕngguhu* and his helpers.

A *sĕngguhu* may perform in a relatively quiet sphere when at the other side of the domestic courtyard only a *wayang lĕmah* is being shown. The performance is more noisy when the *gong* is helping, and bloody when a piglet, held at the hindlegs, is decapitated, with the aim that blood will abundantly flow for the *kala* and *bhuta*. Then on top of this also a cockfight may be arranged for the same purpose; this is not entirely unwelcome to those who produce the cocks and bet on them.

At the occasion of an important ritual, for which the services of several kinds of priests are required, as for instance the inauguration of a regent [47], *abhiséka*, there is a tendency to consider the two kinds of *padanda* as directing themselves to heaven and to sky, and the *sĕngguhu* as specialised in the surface of the earth. Most times, however, he is acting on himself and then one should not be astonished in seeing him *mlaspas*, consecrating any building, just like his colleague the *padanda*. Overlapping of priestly activities is frequent.

Perhaps more frequently than another priest the *sĕngguhu* is invited to consult his WARIGA, either in the form of a treatise on prepared palmleaves or of a board of wood, to find the most suitable day for those ritual activities for which there is a free choice. Whatever the omen of a day, when one has to celebrate a child's perhaps main anniversary, being its reaching the age of $6 \times 5 \times 7$ days (st), there is no escape from that day. But for the celebration of coming of age, of tooth-filing (u), of marriage, of the consecration of a new building or a field for the first time to be used as an irrigated rice-field, evidently the most auspicious day is chosen. Here the *sĕngguhu* is the helping authority.

It is generally known that a Balinese has a keen feeling of direction and feels unhappy when being disorientated. The main sanctuary in the temple should turn its back towards the Great Mountain. When going to sit in the company of a *padanda*, the seat in the east should be kept open for one's Surya. The *sĕngguhu* helps to find the right spot to erect an altar, in the domestic sanctuary as well as in the fields.

His experience is even invoked to detect the localisation of a stolen object.

He may be consulted to state the origin of a person's illness and to fix a method for healing him.

This enumeration of possibilities is far from complete but might give some idea of the help given by this priest to the community as well as to private persons.

13. Priests: Balian

This priest has in common with the *amangku dalang* that he/she operates independently, but whereas *amangku dalang* and *sĕngguhu* are always male, the *balian* frequently is female. *Amangku dalang* and *sĕngguhu* are invited to perform at some spot remote from their house, the *balian* as a rule is consulted at home. Often, but not necessarily, an *amangku dalang* belongs to the caste of the brahmans and the *sĕngguhu* belongs to an intermarrying group, but *balians* appear to start on this career either because they feel attracted to the medical side of *balian*-ship about which Weck wrote a valuable book, or because they had experienced that they could without too much difficulty be brought into a state of trance and then could hear voices, either from the gods or from deified ancestors, with which were helped those who had come to consult them.

In the medical field the *balians* as a rule have a not inconsiderable amount of treatises at their disposal, one of which has the meaningful name: KALI-MAHA-USADHA, 'the great medicine granted by the goddess Kali = Durga'. Other writings deal specially with illnesses of children and may bear the name KANDA MPAT with or without the addition DEWA, god, or BHUTA, or RARE, child. A not inconsiderable part of the cure consists of the muttering of *mantra*, but part of it belongs to medical experience.

It would be too systematical and un-Balinese to make a sharp distinction between the medical and the 'other' activities of the *balian* which belong to widely variegating fields. On my request a neighbour *balian* gave me his calender on which he had noted the activities for which he had been invited long in advance and for which he had found a day, self-evidently a favourable day. His engagements confided to the calender covered one third of the year's days; on top of that he will have fixed several dates in the immediate future, and on top of that he will have been consulted without warning beforehand. Often he had to find a medicine, for children as well as for grown-ups; he found the best place to erect an offering altar in the house-temple as well as in the irrigated field. He consecrated a new building as well as one which had undergone serious repairs. He was consulted about goods which had been lost accidentally as well as about those which might have been stolen. He found the day appropriate for the abduction of a young girl as well as one for the formal conclusion of a marriage. He determined on boundaries and was able to *lukat* soil which had become 'hot' as the consequence of mishap and tresspass (z). He offered *caru* to the netherworldly *bhuta* and *kala*, but *bali/bantĕn* to the gods in the sky. He was in a position to receive a message from the *taksu*, the guardian spirit of the compound, who revealed to him in his trance which medicine to prescribe for a sick person. He even concluded a marriage for which a *sĕngguhu* had fixed the date.

This *balian* cannot complain about being ignored by his co-villagers, as might have been the case when too many of his findings of expert knowledge had turned the wrong way. He is entrusted with the concluding of marriages which, after the preceding elopement, are cases where purification is necessary. But for the remaining dozen or so of rites de passage his help is not invoked. Neither has he anything to do with the ritual for the dead.

14. Priests: Dukuh

Since this introduction tries to approach the problems from the side of the rural population it is justified to begin here by relating that in the few folktales telling about a *dukuh* this priest is mentioned with a respect and cordiality as are not bestowed upon other priests. Judging from their name the *dukuhs* might have been hermits or have lived in new settlements, but in densely populated Bali such circumstances can not be maintained. In the past they must have been more numerous and influential than nowadays, as appears from consulting Balinese literature.

I had an opportunity of visiting one in Karang Asem, the province to which they seem to be confined nowadays, and witnessed his concluding a marriage. He told me that the *dukuhs* were an intermarrying community. Some of them follow the ritual of the padanda Siwa, others that of the padanda Buddha. A treatise dealing with their past and organisation would have been borrowed for consultation by the regent and not yet have been returned. For several reasons it is difficult to travel in Bali so that I did not find an opportunity to see one of the few other *dukuh*, scattered over Karang Asem, the province which has no *sĕngguhu*—there might be a relation between these facts.

No treatise on the care of the dead will go without containing a long *mantra* ascribed to Dukuh Suméru. A writing is ascribed to Dukuh Ampèl Gading, another to Dukuh Krĕtawarsa, to Dukuh Sogra, to Dukuh Suchi-dñana. The GAGURITAN (poem) DUKUH SILADRI, dealing with this hermit, has obtained such a notoriety and belovedness that an author who wished to impart a considerable amount of traditional knowledge to his co-islanders used this title as a frame for a series of not less than ten pamphlets filled with this knowledge.

When the *dukuh* whom I met conducted us for some distance he assured us that he had taken care that we would not be hindered by rain. This ability up to that moment I had only found documented in relation with *dalangs*, for whom it is of the highest importance. It is called *panĕrangan*; *pangujanan*, making of rain is the opposite. The formulas used in this connection are characterised by their presumption. In all other *mantra* the acting priest beseeches, invites and offers, but here he boasts that he is the Omni-potent, able to annihilate this and crush that.

15. Trance

The priests of the preceding paragraphs are mediators between the gods and mankind, aware of its frailty and lack of mastery of the means by which the Gods wish to be approached. Numerous as these mediators are, various as are the *mantra*, *mudra* and *yadña* with which they work, different as are the fields in which they deploy their capabilities—in times of crisis and urgency the will of God must be felt, His words (be it not His voice) must be heard, a decision must be reached, no longer by using priestly channels but by listening to a medium in a state of trance.

When for a temple festival pure water is fetched from the *béji*, source, and the cortege which has gone to obtain it is approaching the temple, it is welcomed by another cortege having gone to meet it. Both groups start to dance, while slowly moving in the direction of the temple. Nobody seems to wonder when one or more of the dancers after some time gets into a mild state of trance.

In the temple itself, frequently during the night, a woman falls into a trance and reveals the deity's wishes [6].

Immediately after the most recent *puputan* (bringing to an end, sc. of an armed conflict), the cremation of Jaya Prana, the innocent victim of his feudal lord's jealousy, was ordered to be organised by the medium of trance. This happened in the northern corner of the island but found an enormous response everywhere. During the following years night after night trance dances were held in South Bali and must have given consolation to nervous minds [21].

One might have expected that priesthood frowned upon direct contact with the gods and its ignoring the priests' intermediating position. To the contrary: the priests do not scorn trance, but *pamangku* and *padanda* do their utmost best to make return to ordinary life him or her who is tired to death after having been under the spell of the god. Popular, frequent and frightful are the dances of the mythological quadruped *barong* and the evil witch Chalon Arang, at the end of which a number of men in a trance direct the tips of their creeses against their own breasts. *Pamangkus* assist them with *toya*; this never fails [4].

It is only self-evident that not all exhibitions of trance are always a full hundred procent genuine. They prove, however, that the Balinese, in their craving for guidance and being possessed by the gods, to a considerable extent have institutionalised these happenings and are helped by them in their difficulties of life.

16. Laymen

The repeated mentioning of different kinds of priests might have suggested that they only are the active part of society in matters of religion and that the ordinary people, the laymen, are merely passive. But this is far from reality. A good mother—and few Balinese girls escape motherhood or would aspire to that situation—is aware of the *kanda mpat* as we have seen (c). Daily she has to prepare her small plaited offerings, adorned with petals, substantiated by some grains of rice. In most cases they are offered to the gods and therefore should be called *bali* or *bantěn*; the gods, however, have only a limited time to enjoy the *sari*, essence, of the offering, for the pigeons are used to time and place of edibles. Sometimes the offerings, not unfrequently consisting of some fish or meat and accompanied by some drops of alcoholic drink, now called *caru*, are offered to the netherworldly *bhuta* and *kala*, who equally must take the profit of a few seconds only, for after that the ever-hungry Balinese dogs enjoy their leavings (o 5). The trees in the courtyard get their share, and probably more important but less visible are the offerings indoors for the images of the Goddess Sri and her spouse Sadana, made of coins, who take care of the welfare of the family (r). A few feet above a baby's cot is hung a nicely-carved and brightly pictured small contraption, made to contain offerings for the god Kumara, himself ever young, who bestows his cares upon babies. Some spots in the domestic shrine have to be furnished with daily offerings, but the trees only periodically are adorned with offerings.

But most offerings, perhaps, are needed for the irrigated ricefields (a, b 1). This staple food requires constant care during the several stages of its growth, flowering, development of seed and harvest; each stage needs its own offerings. Cool reasoning points to the importance of the waterworks, for lack of water in due time means a diminished harvest or even no harvest at all, so that waterdivisions and watershed receive their own offerings.

17. Humble Things

Sufficiently visible in many a kitchen are the kitchen gods (q 2), of about the same one foot size and the same material, clay, as the Malipa and Malipi displayed at the celebration of *bajang cholong*, the half-a-year anniversary of a young child (t 2). The kitchen gods may go for years, Malipa and Malipi only for a few hours.

For the *taksu*, lord and guardian of the temple territory, a small pavilion is a necessary feature of every temple. *Ngrurah* is the lord of the soil; on approaching an important temple one may leave his offering for him on a large piece of stone (q 5), rounded off by centuries of movement in the waters, the same kind as that used at the end of *nigang sasihin* and covering the afterbirth. When in a temple offerings are laid on top of it, they are reputed for Ibu Pěrtiwi, Mother Earth (q 5). At the Pura Luhur of Batu Karu the debris of sacred buildings, which should not be consumed by fire, are collected in a pit; their Guardian is Jro Bangbang, Mister Pit [22].

Déwi Malanting receives offerings from all those engaged in commerce, shopkeeping and marketing.

Mainly for lack of a good heading to deal with the following subject it will be incorporated here. In North Bali, the province Bulèlèng, everybody knew about existence of the were-tigers of Pulaki. As recently as 1949 they paid worship to the material remains of Jaya Prana, in the past the victim of his feudal lord's jealousy, now the symbol of the victims of resistance. In august he was to be cremated, his symbolic body and the offerings were outspread on a bamboo scaffolding. On the evening preceding the cremation, during hours at a stretch, silently the "Invisibles" passed under the construction made for Jaya Prana; all those present were awe-struck by the perception. The "Invisibles" at that occasion made it abundantly clear that they did not merely belong to the lore, told to the young children by old nannies [21].

Whether one travels by coach or by truck, the Balinese driver will have provided himself with petrol as well as with at least one offering. When reaching the watershed between south and north Bali, he stops a few seconds, giving his helper an opportunity to put a small offering in the pillar destined for this purpose, accompanied by a short prayer. The same is done when passing the cave of bats. When the vehicle has to take a risk on a spot of possible danger, a small offering is needed.

All these daily and periodical offerings ask for time and attention, but are surpassed by far by the number and size of the offerings needed for rites de passage, those for the *bhuta* and above all for the dead at the occasion of a cremation (e, o, p, q). It will be evident that the average inhabitant of an island provided with some twenty thousand temples has a life busy with running after his religious duties. Has he time, thought and energy left for speculation and theology? The author of 'Religion of Java', Clifford Geertz, when writing about Bali, where repeatedly he did research, found that the Balinese priest with his *mantra, mudra, rajah* (drawing) and *yadña* is stronger in ortho-praxis than in ortho-doxy. For large sections of the population this judgment might be justified.

On the other hand: at least half of the books published in Bali during the last quarter of a century are in the field of religion and philosophy. The ethical prescriptions of the SARA-SAMUCCHAYA [42] have even been published by three different publishers. This points in the direction of constant demand, and as may be assumed, not only by the clergy but also by laymen.

18. Rites de Passage

Some attention has been given to the worship of the gods and some to the buying off of the *bhuta* and *kala*, which is frequently accompanied by killing of victims. *Balians* are undemanding when they separate the head of a small chicken from its body followed by tearing off the legs. In Bali one must grow up with the spearing of a chicken or a pig from bottom to beak and be accustomed to the thought that the separated head with open eyes of one of Bali's lovely cows or calves, frisky like deer, lying on the ground, is welcome to *kala-bhuta* and welfare-bringing to mankind. But offerings for the wellbeing of the little ones and of human beings in general are perhaps less bloody and in any case more jocular and carefree.

Though after the Pacific War the *padandas* and *ulakas* constituted their organisation and held their conferences and Government instituted provincial offices for religious affairs and even a central one in Denpasar, there is not yet a universal series of *manusa-yadña*. The differences, however, are of no importance. It makes no difference whether one begins with marriage followed by the celebration of the first signs of gravidity or begins with them to end with marriage, as long as the odd fifteen in between are more or less the same. As the rituals to be performed are aiming at the welfare of the young baby or the child, as much as possible the help of a priest is invoked by the loving parents, as a rule a *pamangku*. There is birth and the falling off of the umbilical cord and the celebration of having reached the age of seven plus five days; at none of these (and the following) days the parents will forget the offerings to the child's four elder brothers or sisters, the *kanda mpat*.

Now follows five times seven plus seven, makes forty two days, when the young mother is in the centre of attention. On her behalf an offering is made in the nearest streaming water, said to represent the Hindu God Wisnu, and in the kitchen, being the site of fire, the Hindu Agni/Gĕni=Brahma. Cortege, children dressed up, the end of actual and ritual impurity.

But the festivity which most of all is mentioned in the padandas' calendars is that celebrated when the child has reached the age of three months of 5 × 7 days. Known as *nigang sasihin* or *nĕlu bulanin* after this number, but also as *nyambutin*, 'taking up (the baby, which allegedly had been taken away) and *bajang cholong*, 'stolen baby', it combines quite a number of picturesque usages (s).

The first episode finds place near a streaming water where we find, stretched out on their backs, the clay figurines of a male and a female called Malipa and Malipi (t 2), representing most probably the parents of a substitute baby, *bajang cholong*. After a ritual during a quarter of an hour they are left on their places; the scene of activities is now the domestic courtyard. Much attention is given to that bajang cholong in the form of a young coconut but in the end it is buried outside the main gate. The real baby is now adorned with silver or even gold rings around pulses and ankles. It is for the first time brought into contact with the earth (s 3), a ritual which in the Javanese Principalities too was celebrated. In Kalimantan of old the boy child of a chief with his feet touched iron and stone, the head of a killed fuffalo and of a killed slave. This usage is neither Muslim nor Hindu but precedes both religions.

In Bali the baby is kept under the plaited basket which serves to give a fighting cock the pleasure of looking at the passers-by, but now it is called *sok suddha-mala*, 'cleansed of impurities', but meant is: 'cleaning from impurities' (s, t 2). The baby is kept on the lap of a small child which has not yet changed teeth, sitting on a stone in a hole in the ground. Its hand is kept in the water of a basin and helped to fish up small golden fish, a sure sign that in the course of his life he will be able to look after himself and make his fortune (s).

As for this occasion an elaborate and expensive set of offerings has been made, the preceding ritual activities, promoting the baby's welfare, are combined with the name-giving and even the first ritual haircutting (t 3, t 4), which according to some authors should only be celebrated when the child is not 105 days old but 210, or even some time after that, but before the appearance of the first tooth.

A girl's first menses should be celebrated, and not long afterwards her teeth should be filed (u), though frequently toothfiling is postponed till marriage, this first or last of the so-called *manusa-yadña*, offerings for the sake of mankind.

The preceding paragraphs are only meant to suggest that in Bali various stages of human development are accompanied by priestly activities because they are said to be religious duties. Superfluous to say that at any of the occasions one set of offerings is destined for the *kanda mpat*.

As the cost of the prescribed offerings in many a case proves to be prohibitive, frequently a stage of development is ignored. But then at a later occasions, for instance at *nĕlu bulanin*, the parents make up for the arrears. Far from thinking: 'the child has passed safely into next stages without trouble and expense and that is that', there appears to be a lively feeling that debts to the gods should be paid. The costs of *yadña*, offerings, determine whether a ritual can be held or not.

19. Burial and Cremation (v, w, x)

It is only natural that *manusa-yadña*, 'offerings for the living', rites de passage, is follwed by *pitra-yadña*, 'care of the dead'. When compared with India and its Hinduism the rites de passage show only a limited conformity: on death-ritual we must say: The result of blending more than a milennium of Hinduism with the preceding milennia of inter-insular antique Indonesian religion shows a remarkable tenacity of the last-mentioned and limited progress of Hinduism.

Indian climate and Hinduism ask cremation immediately after death. The Balinese were used to burial or exposure, but their lords were keen on festivities and ceremonies in honour of their dead parents and relatives, be it that they were not in a hurry. The penetration of Hinduism has resulted in most cases in cremation of those whose heritage proved or promised to be sufficient to that purpose, but as a rule it is a matter of months if not years before taking place. Some more well-to-do people in the meantime do not bury the dead person but place him on a bier in a separate building. In most cases he is buried and dug up, in reality or symbolically, and by far most people are never cremated at all.

According to popular belief the spirit of the dead lead a restless existence. They roam around especially on their graveyard and are irritable because of their not yet having reached their final stage and are in need of offerings (*tarpana*, 'giving satisfaction'). But when the *padanda* has started with the preparations for cremation, more is needed, to wit *panĕbusan*, redemption of the soul from *patala*, that is hell. Another conception, found in the manuals of the *padandas*, is the union of the soul with that of the *badawang*, tortoise of the underworld, frequently found in stone sculpture, serving as the base of a *méru*.

Dead bodies and effigies could be burned by themselves, but as a rule relatives and heirs do their utmost best to cremate their dead in material surroundings up to their position in life. A *padanda* should be cremated in a bamboo contraption looking like a *padmasana*. Lions and bulls are for the dead of the second caste, *mérus* are used for those of lower status and the number of tiers is a delicate affair. Commoners are frequently cremated in fishlike coffins; there are still more possibilities.

On the open air crematorium the soil must be purified ritually before the arrival of the funeral cortege, which in its course always evokes much hilarity. The final purification of the dead body is due to the Holy Waters and the Fire. Ashes are confided to streaming water, considered to conduct them to the sea.

The first cremation is not the end of the ritual for the dead. At least a second one should follow, after twelve days. It may last years before the expensive last one is held, at which then not only the soul is granted its final liberation but at which its *kanda mpat* share the same privilege.

Where does the soul go? To heaven, to begin with, but since the Balinese have several juxta-posed and super-imposed heavens, according to an existent manual on care of the dead, it depends on the length of a formula spoken by the *padanda* in which heaven one comes to enjoy a new life. Perhaps this idea is old-fashioned now; death-ritual is in movement. Some treatises prescribe the same ritual as that which a new priest undergoes at consecration but others have struck it.

After a sojourn in heaven one is reborn and in a historical writing we find an expression of the grief of children at discovering the fact that their parents have been reborn as leeches (y). Their preceding life on earth will have suggested this result. This application of the law of *karma* makes an Indian impression but typical Balinese is the thought that frequently one is reborn in the circle of the blood-relatives. Then the consulting of a *balian* will reveal which grandparent's soul has found its site in the baby asked about.

Judging from the manuals of the *padandas* these priests strive to give complete liberation and vanishment to the souls.

As a rule a Balinese is an agriculturist, living in a compound on which he has several buildings. There is always a separate corner, his house-temple, where he worships those forbears who as a result of cremation have become gods. A man of some means has a special pavilion in which to put a corpse on its bier before burial or cremation.

20. The Playful Mind

The Balinese gods are unreservedly pleased with all fields of art. They love music and have a fine ear, so that for different occasions different melodies must be played and even completely different orchestras are needed. The worship of the dead asks for other instruments than the celebration of the anniversary of a temple. The gods, moreover, are fond of the theatrical performances and dances to which the *pamangku* has invited them. Religion in Bali stimulates the arts, those better known just mentioned as well as the lesser known of making offerings.

The greater part of the Balinese daily offerings consist of some plaited trifle, made from some strips of palmleaf, frequently with some cuttings giving it a more outspoken shape, a few petals and a few grains of rice. Such a gadget is a pleasure for the eye, for the gods as well as for us. A Balinese housewife has to make number of them, daily. As soon as a special offering has to be made, be it for gods or *bhutas*, mankind or the forbears, the *tukangs bantĕn*, makers of offerings, know exactly what is needed and how much. The existing description of a *lis* gives an idea of the complicated nature of one object used during Balinese ritual. One should see the huge offerings and get an explanation of all parts and subdivisions. They have to be made from their prescribed materials, there are rules for their number, their colour, their direction, their function. The *tukangs bantĕn*, usually elderly ladies belonging to the caste of the brahmans, enjoy the time of their life when they have the responsibility for the offerings for an important ceremony. They know and are consulted by those less experienced [28].

Collecting the necessary ingredients and plaiting of baskets begins weeks beforehand and fills the minds with joyful expectation. Limited is the number of countries where the anniversary of St. Nicholas is celebrated on the eve of december the sixth, less limited that where a Christmas tree is provided with candles and presents. The great Balinese offerings upon me make the impression of the joy and display of originality as in a combination of celebrations of Christmas with St. Nicholas. Perhaps because the offerings are deteriorating rashly and are superabundant in number and endless in variation they have not yet been studied as to their meaning, but this is evident that artistic invention and freedom have found possibilities here.

The necessarily short remarks on the playful mind in Balinese religion have found their place here because in the ritual for the dead several details are so eminently expressive. Even the lay relatives of the dead person must hear and understand the *padanda* when with a booming voice he invites the soul of the dead man in the building opposite him to approach, to wash the feet and rinse the mouth, to eat, to drink and finally to enjoy a betel quid. In the case of periodical *tarpana*, giving satisfaction to the soul, this is the end and the soul is bound to retake its erring course after this treat. Only a few hours before cremation the formulas ensuring accession to heaven, complete redemption and extinction are added to the ones mentioned above.

The soul does not go empty-handed on its long and far way. It is provided with a small stick to lean on and it is given three feather-light writings by way of passport and safe-conduct; they are called *raca-dana, ulantaga* or *walantaka* and *pripih,* this last one made of sandalwood or even gold.

In the *mantras* helping the soul a huge *kukupu,* butterfly, is mentioned more than once, assumedly as its conveyance or as its own shape, to make the flight possible, but more often *titiran,* a bird with the size of a dove.

Before cremation during the night a *damar kurung,* Chinese lantern, is hung near the entrance of the courtyard of the person to be cremated. In the immediate neighbourhood of the remains another light, *angĕnan* or *hrĕdaya* shows the way to the erring soul, displaying a soft light through an egg-shell.

The soul may have been delivered from its earthly bonds but it has not become omniscient, so that it must be pointed to the dangers on its way. In a long *mantra* it is told never to take southwesterly direction, that of *krodha,* anger, for that leads to hell. Having arrived in 'Flower Quarter' it should not pick flowers for then the heavenly nymphs would punish it. It receives instruction how to pass another danger: the wobbling bridge. And the ninefold gate. And so on.

Another manual tells the soul in great detail how the horrors of the hereafter are parts of his own body: the sharp grasses are his hairs, the wobbling bridge is his tongue, the huge pieces of rock playing snap shut are his lips—in this way the limbs etc. are equated to the whole inventory of hellish terrors.

Infinitely charming is one of the forms of *pĕgat,* 'cutting (the liens)', 'taking leave'. A young child had died; it lay on its bier. Her playmates were at the foot end, and connected with it by strings which they held in their hands. Midway each string was a coin which in Bali has a hole in the middle. Such a string was burned through at the bier side of the coin so that each child received its coin as a souvenir. Play? Fancy? Extremely touching.

The examples could be multiplied but the matter is sufficiently clear. Inseparable union of seriousness and playful phantasy.

But what to think when *déwa* and *bhatara* are the word for deity and God, but also used as a feudal title and the word used to address the king?

Priests and laymen agree that teeth should be filed at maturity 'to prevent that one should be reborn provided with fangs and tusks'. One never saw anybody, his mouth adorned in this way, but knows that not everybody had his teeth filled. The costs for the offerings considered to be needed at tooth-filing are often prohibitive. Here a possible former belief seems to have ceded its place to social play, the tooth-filing display of wealth.

The dead should be cremated, 'to save their souls'. The ritual is expensive and by far most Balinese are never cremated. Are the Balinese so cruel or is cremation more a matter of social display than of belief? Some say: potlatch.

I witnessed a commoner's marriage. First there was a long palaver between all men concerned at such an occasion; each had his say, some of them at considerable length.

The results were found to be satisfactory; without delay bride and groom went through several picturesque practical rituals. At the right moment the bride took leave from her parental home and was genuinely moved to tears. Next the offerings were brought for the first signs of gravidity; such things happen. But then the three children came to the front for since several years the couple had been happily married. The whole performance had mainly been a social play: the groom had found the money for the offerings for his marriage. Now he could be sure of his voting right in the village community.

21. Cows—Not Holy

In India cows should be respected, never be killed and eaten. In Bali the most attractive cattle, coloured and agile like deer, are reared for agricultural help and finally for the slaughterhouses of Singapore and exceptionally for offerings. The offerings for the gods may consist of flowers, fruits and cereal products, and some fowl, but those for the numerous and ever-hungry *bhuta* and *kala* can contain scores of different animals. These victims are recompensated, however, for the *padanda* in a long prayer gives them the assurance that they will be reborn in a much better state.

Rebirth in the own greater family, learned from a *balian* in a state of trance is an idea not borrowed from Hinduism. Temples consisting of open courts instead of closed buildings, gods living above the great mountain and the lakes but not day and night present in the temple—those are conceptions not found in Indian Hinduism. Cremation as a matter of social position and not of belief is alien to Indian Hinduism. The preponderant importance attached to the Holy Waters in their great variety is typically Balinese too; it lead to the terminology *agama tirtha,* the religion of Holy Water. The luxurious and charming but oppressive growth of offerings and their influence seems to be alien to Indian Hinduism.

Nobody can object when this artistic and thus playful population claims Hinduism as its religion. One can only admire their wisdom in denoting their religion as agama Hindu Bali, Balinese Hinduism.

LEGENDS TO THE ILLUSTRATIONS

(a) Offerings in the paddies, for the young rice-seedlings, recently transplanted from their nursery, should be brought everywhere. Note that some are on the ground (*caru*), destined for the netherworldly beings (bhuta-kala) with the intention that they will be satisfied, will do no harm and retire. Those on the platform (*bantĕn*) are destined for the gods, especially the goddess Sri. Note also the hanging offering of plaited palmleaves.

(b 1) Landscape with (partially brick) offering niche. Unless clouds cover the mountains, their chain is always visible.

(b 2) Puri Mayun at Mĕngwi. The mérus, pagodas, have 3, 5, 7, 9, 11 tiers (tumpangs) according with the respect due to the person in whose honour they have been erected.

(c 1) Kanda Mpat, the four elder brothers/sisters, to the both sides of younger brother [5].

(c 2) The same beings, but now stark naked.

(c 3) Repentant four first-born heavenly seers Kursika-Garga-Métri-Kurusya, paying homage to the Supreme Lord; forgiven they return to East-South-West-North as the gods Iswara-Brahma-Mahadéwa-Wisnu, recognizable by their weapons.

(d 1) Kamaligi is the name of an offering brought at padudusan, lustration, of the Bauddhas.

(d 2) Cock, drake and young boar are able to pick and eat away the human defilements in the beginning of the ceremony of padudusan.

(d 3) Zodiac-beaker, prasèn, specially used for purification.

(d 4) Vehicle for the godly ones.

(e) Yama-raja, drawing by Ida Wayan Raja (Griya Tĕngah, Bodha Kling, Karang Asĕm) and sculpture in Puri Kaba-Kaba, Tabanan. Note the four surrounding flat stones and all their offerings. For application of the letters cf. 'Agama Tirtha' [22].

ni	ra	ra	ja	sa
ya	ma	ma	mé	do
ncha	sa	ya	mé	do
ra	ma	da	da	ro
ya	ni	ya	ya	da

ni	ra ma	ja
yo da	ya	mé do
?	ksa ya	sa

(f 1) Bhuta sungsang. Bhuta on itself is already bad enough; topsy turvy is worse still, just like an anti-clockwise going round.

(f 2) Chalon Arang, the bad witch, dancing with her disciples, as portrayed by the famous artist Sobrat.

(g 1) Sculpture of a guardian with his back turned to a wall.

(g 2) Durgā Mahiṣāsura-mardinī, Durga dancing on back of bull, crushing his demon. Found on hill Kutri in Gianyar. Cf. Dr. W. F. Stutterheim, 'Oudheden van Bali I'; Tekst 1929, Platen 1930, uitgegeven door de Kirtya Liefrinck-Van der Tuuk, Singaradja, Bali, This Durga might portray the mother of King Erlangga who married a Javanese princess.

(g 3) The benevolent god Wisnu, mounted on his vehicle, the awe-inspiring bird Garuda. Note the polèng cloth adorning the sculpture.

(g 4) This sculpture on a cross-road has as his function to deter the god Kala in particular and the bhuta-kala in general. Like (g 1) he is weaponed with a kind of sabre, whereas g 3 manipulates a (ritual) bell. A priest's bell as its handle has a vajra, thunderbolt. The padanda Bodha, Buddhist brahman priest, on top of that handles a double vajra as a ritual instrument. It makes all the difference whether during his ritual he worships and invites the celestial gods, using a flower, or tries to chase off the netherworldly bhuta-kala by means of bell (provided with bajra) and (double) bajra.

(h) Various karang, mankind is afraid of meeting on his way (a century ago collected by Dr. H. N. van der Tuuk, accessible in Leiden University Library). 1) k. lawéyan (trunk). 2) kuwuk (tiger-cat). 3. tmaja (scorpion). 4) katunggèng (scorpion). 5) bĕbĕtukan (evil spirit of the cemetery). 6) Ludra (the most dreaded god of the South-West).

(i) 1) rangda (the frightful widow-witch Chalon Arang). 2) domba (ram). 3) bawi (boar). 4) rarangut (a kind of animal). 5) sarpa (serpent-king). 6) baduda (dung-beetle). 7) bintulu (yaksa, attendant on the god of wealth).

(j) Tumbal rajah, drawings of counter-magic. 1) t.r.ukur (effigy, cf. Wirz No. 52). 2) t.r.ĕntud-ĕntud ('knees', and the knee *is* in the middle, but we call it a *leg* with a head on top of it). 3) t.r.tuñjung bang tuñjung putih (red lotus white lotus —unclear). 4) no caption given. 5) t.r.tangan-tangan (hands, yes, but ringfinger changing into underleg, that in upperleg, that in terrific head). 6) t.r.Yama-raja, anggèn pangijĕng goyu (?) (a means to protect little children against horrifying léyak). t.r.tumbal bongol (?). 8) t.r.lulut (attachment, devotion).

(k 1) Pamangku in prayer with his offerings; notice his mudra [38].

(k 2) Five pamangkus officiating together; variety of offerings.

(k 3) Pamangku dancing, at the head of a cortege.

(k 4) Pamangku officiating; right hand: flower; left hand: bell.

(k 5) Humble place of worship in the fields.

(m 1) Two padandas officiating simultaneously. The surroundings are unusual; the ritual is not that of daily preparation of Holy Water but so important that donning of mitre and strings of beads is necessary.

(m 2) The padanda's (chief) wife should learn to perform the same rituals as he himself. She is consecrated at the same time as he [2] and, when officiating, is characterised by a remarkable headdress.

(m 3) Some offerings are piled up as high/tall as a man.

(n 1) A performance of wayang lĕmah, shadow theatre on the ground, not for the pleasure of humans but for the placation of the superhumans. The puppet in the centre, standing on one foot (éka-pāda) only is Tintiya (a-chintya = a-cintya = He Who cannot be imagined). Behind Him the kakayon or gunungan (tree-group or mountain-group), used for marking the different acts.

(n 2, 4) Same. There is no screen; the puppets are leaning against a thread, stretched between two branches of the dapdap-tree, symbol of undestructibility.

(n 3) A pĕndasar or pĕnasar, 'basic puppet', one of the four, Twalèn. Notice his girdle; the patron of blocks, black-grey-white, called polèng, is a prerogative for exceptional persons and exceptional circumstances. As a rule it points to his bearer's flying capacity or other supernatural power.

(o 1) Relatives and neighbours cooperate in the preparation of the numerous offerings.

(o 2) Great is the variety of the elaborate offerings for the gods.

(o 3) Remarkable are the gayah, made of pork, partially representing the sĕnjata, weapons or emblems of the gods of the nine directions (E-S-W-N-SE-SW-NW-NE-Centre), called nawa-sanga, 'nine-nine'.

(o 4) As soon as a caru, offering to the netherworldly beings has been brought,

(o 5) A dog is allowed to eat them, leaving little time to bhutas and kalas.

(p 1) Whole roasted pigs constitute offerings; they are packed in palm leaves.

(p. 2) Innumerable cookies/pastries are made from dough; here some more elaborate creations.

(p 3) These offerings, hanging from a platform, are called sampéyan and sĕntèg.

(p. 4) On top of the offering altar: bantĕn panglĕmijian. On top of the plaited basket: bantĕn pamrayaschitta, serving as an expiation for involuntary shortcomings.

(q 1) At the occasion of a celebration, a sculpture of profane exterior is adorned with a white headdress (as worn by officiating pamangkus and their helpers) and polèng cloth; the temporary altar in front of him gives room for many offerings.

(q 2) The female one of our pair of kitchen gods, outside her domain.

(q 3) This mythological pair of animals gets its offerings.

(q 4) The dog on his pedestal is not forgotten in the round of offerings.

(q 5) This large stone, representing Mother Earth, shares in the offerings.

(r 1) Sadana and Sri, the god and the goddess of wealth, consist mainly of jinah bolong, coin with a hole, with the exception of the faces which are made of wood. They are two-dimensional, as here, but exist also in three-dimensional form.

(r 2) The déwa Sang Hyang Sadana as found in 'SUNAR AGAMA, tjara melakukan upatjara hari raya Hindu Bali' oleh I Kĕtut Bangbang Gdé Rawi, Balimas, Denpasar, 1956.

(s 1) Rarègèk, a spookish creation, made of plaited palmleaves, used at the celebration of a baby's having reached the age of $3 \times 5 \times 7 = 105$ days = half an oton (year) of 210 days. Perhaps none of the other dozen or so rites de passage is being celebrated with so much gusto and so much variation. The rarègèk is only known from North Bali.

(s 2) The sok suddha-mala is plentifully provided with offerings on top.

(s 3) The baby under (the protection of) the sok suddha-mala for the first time in his life is made to touch Mother Earth.

(s 4) The baby (not without some guidance and help) 'spontaneously' succeeds in fishing up with his right hand some precious (silver, gold) trinkets, found on the bottom of the earthenware basin, filled with water, on top of which he is being kept. In this way he proves to be able to gain richess in his life.

(t 1) The offerings necessary for the celebration of nigang sasihin are being blessed here.

(t 2) The ritual of nigang sasihin begins at the bank of a streaming water. Two clay puppets of an unmistakable male and female appearance are indispensable.

(t 4) A baby's first haircutting should be performed ceremoniously. Apart from the scissors, gunting, visible in (t 3), the officiating priest uses (from right to left) a lotosbud, a kalpika provided with a ruby and a pancha-kosika.

(t 3) During the hair-cutting not the own mother keeps the baby on her lap.

(t 5) Offering at the occasion of tooth-filing (cf. bed to the right).

(u 1) Filing of teeth is preceded by prayer to Smara, god of love.

(u 2) After having been submitted to the filing of the teeth.

(u 3) A look in the mirror may give reason for satisfaction.

(u 4) Hammer and chisel are used as well as the file (u 5).

(v 1) Cremation as a rule only takes place months if not years after death; the remains then often are reduced to a bare minimum, bundled together in cloth, white and canary-yellow, called sĕkah, 'flower'. In view of the high costs of a cremation sometimes scores of people are cooperating.

(v 2) This 'bull' is destined to contain dozens of sĕkah and to be cremated with them.

(v 3) Woman bearing angĕnan according to Wirz, hṛdaya according to my Southern informant.

(v 4) A nine tiers' méru being carried to the cemetery/burning ground.

(w 1) The remains of a person dead since several years are ceremoniously being dug up.

(w 2) Cremation animals are not indispensable; this is a simple cremation. It should be noted that nobody is dressed up; everybody wears his ordinary clothes.

(w 3) After cremation: ashes laid out in human form and adorned with offerings.

(w 4) The remaining bones of the person mentioned in (w 1) are carefully lain together as a preparatory step leading to cremation.

(x 1) Cremation bulls may have a fierce appearance, nearly challenging.

(x 2) But still the flames will consume them. Note box with remains under belly.

(x 3) A turret, mainly for artistic purposes, destined to be burned.

(x 4) Shrines for ancestors in a domestic sanctuary of nobility.

(y 1) Polychrome cotton cloth depicting the hereafter with its hellish cauldron in the centre.

(y 2) The same, but the cauldron, called tambra go-mukha, 'the bronze (cauldron) with the cowheads', now bottom left.

(z 1) One should make this drawing when soil proves to belong to 'lĕmah sanggar' [25] and 'hot'. When some specified offerings are added, the result should be perfect.

(z 2) Tumbal rajah (cf. j) Sang Hyang Ulu (Divine Head), to be used as pripèn, safe-conduct given to the soul of the dead after it has been provided with toya pangĕntas, 'water shipping it over'.

ILLUSTRATIONS

Offerings (to the ricegoddess)

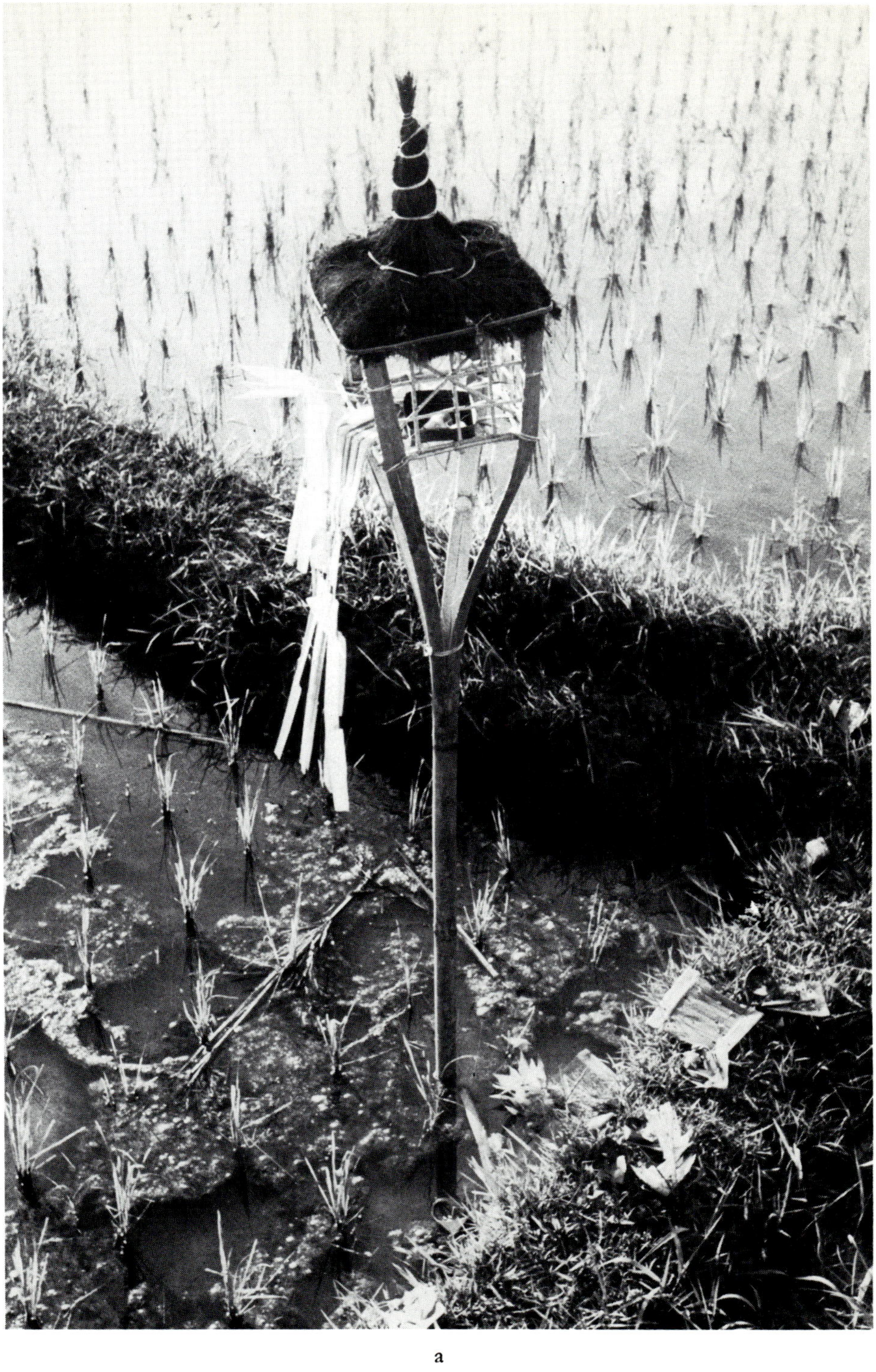

a

Offerings (to the ricegoddess)

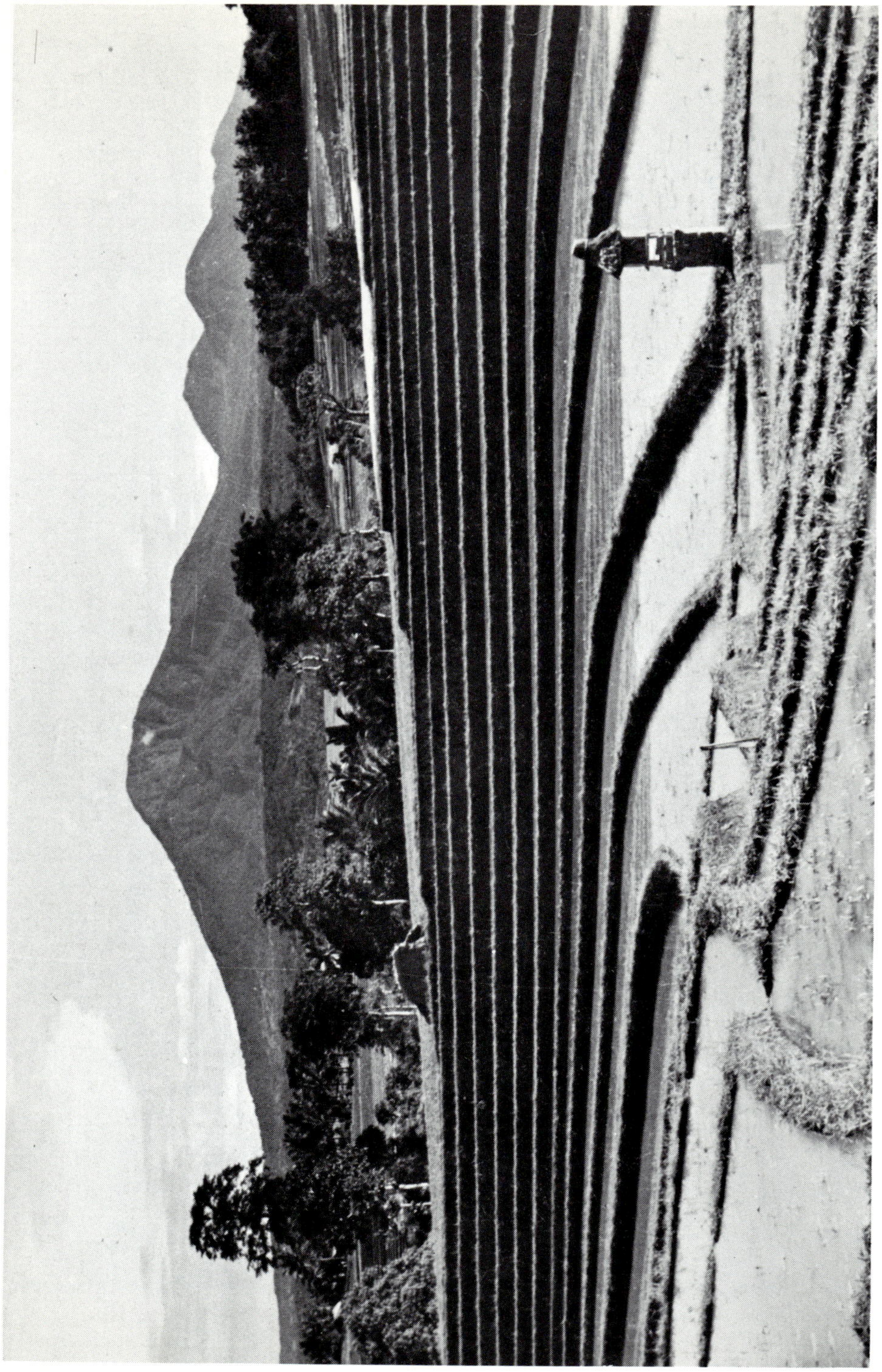

b1

Mérus in Mengwi

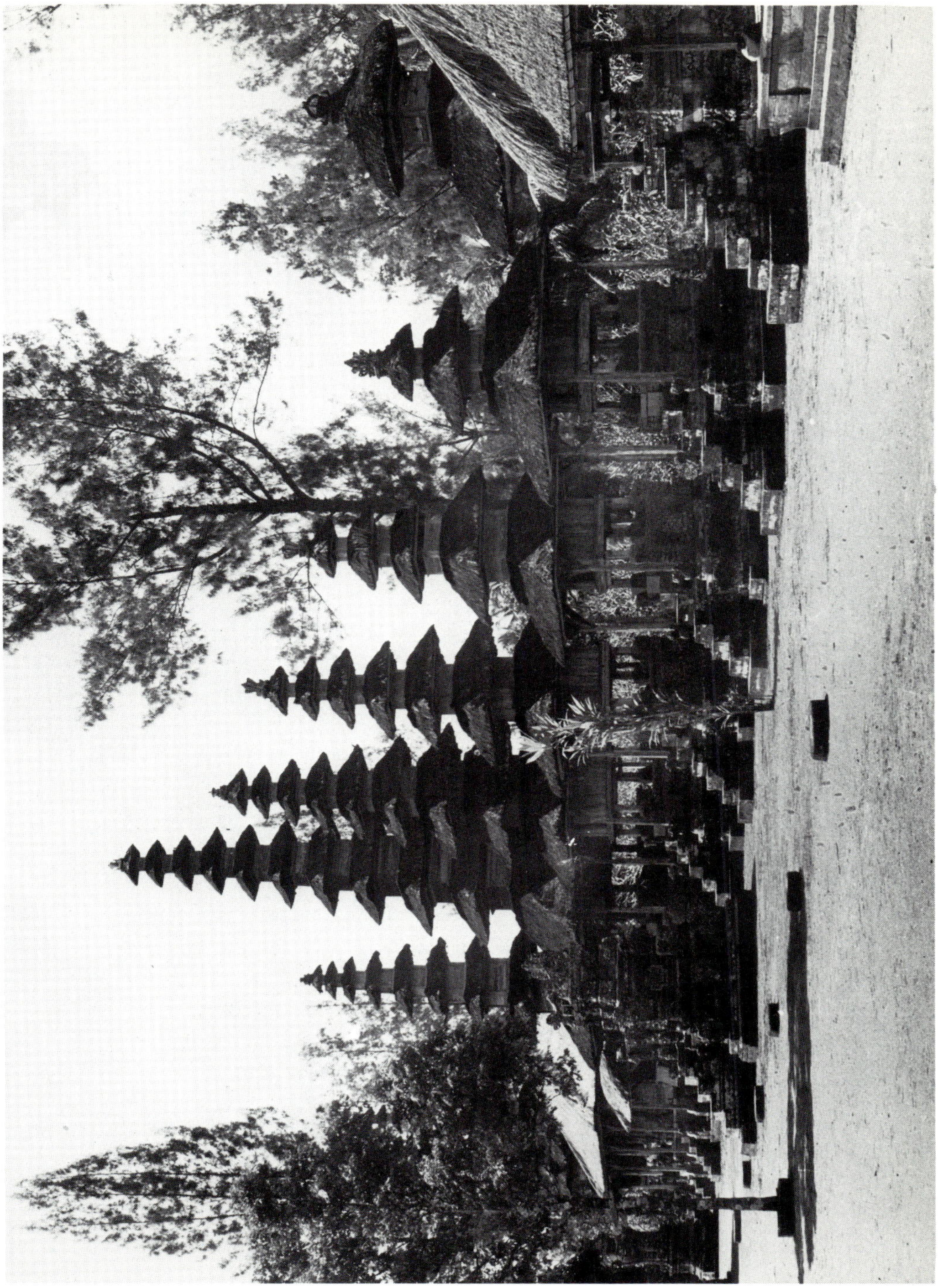

b 2

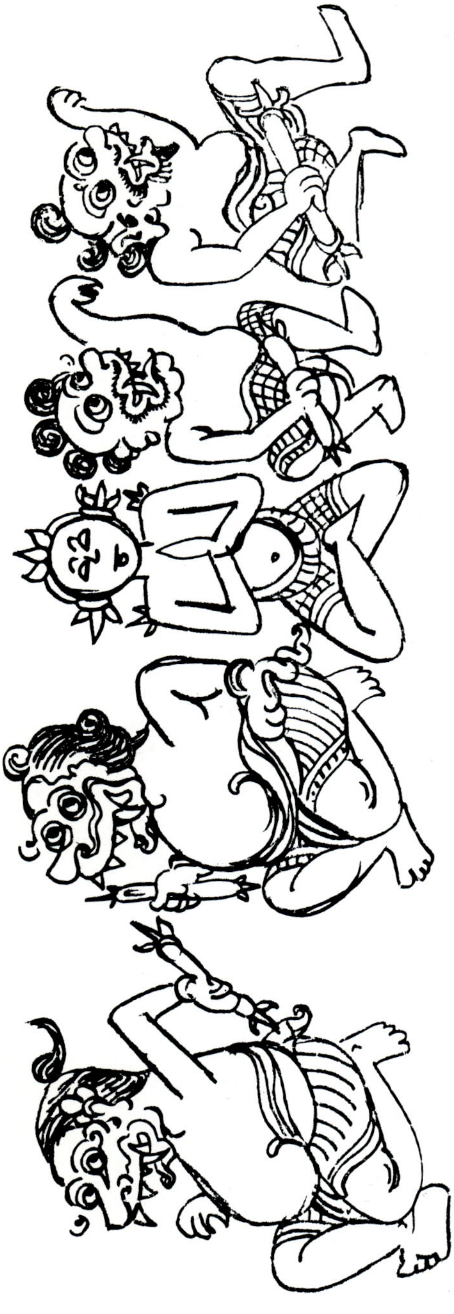

c 1

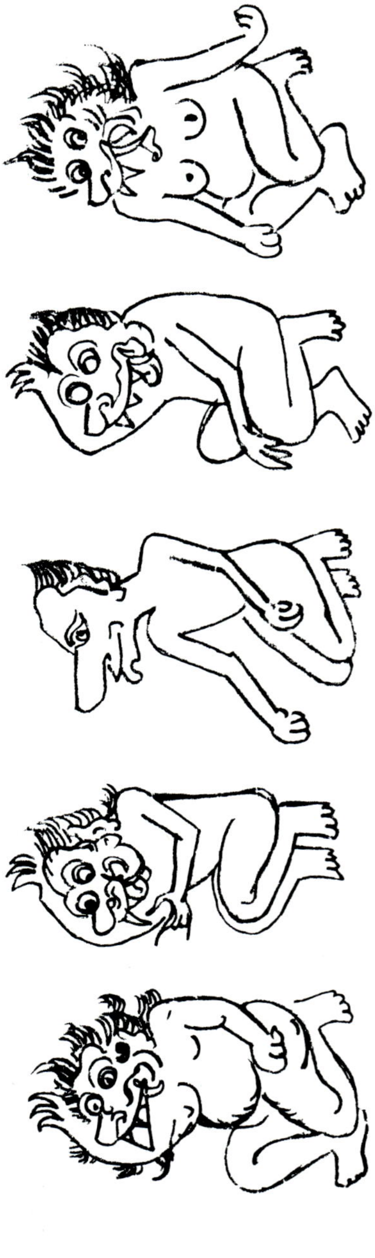

c 2

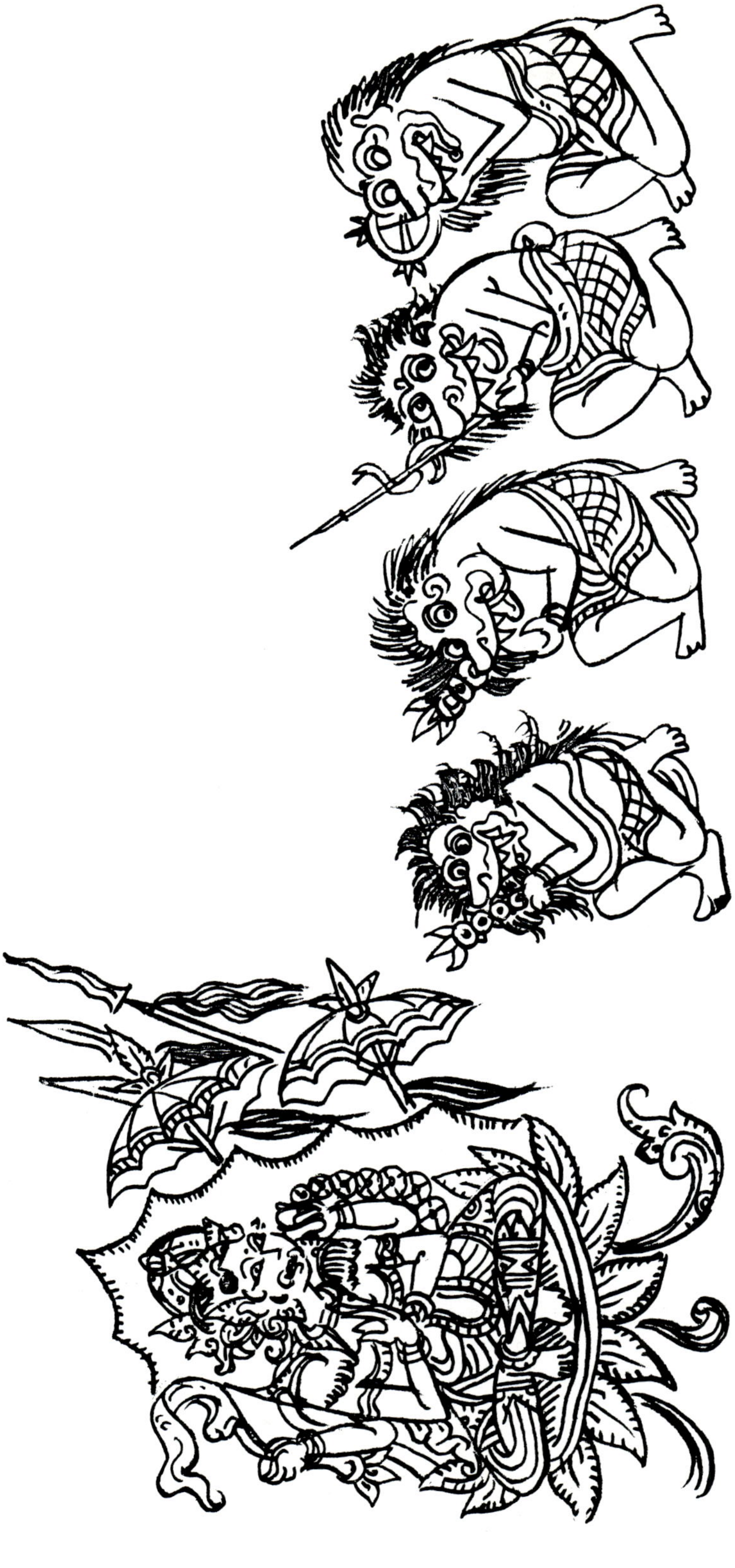

c 3

Lustration

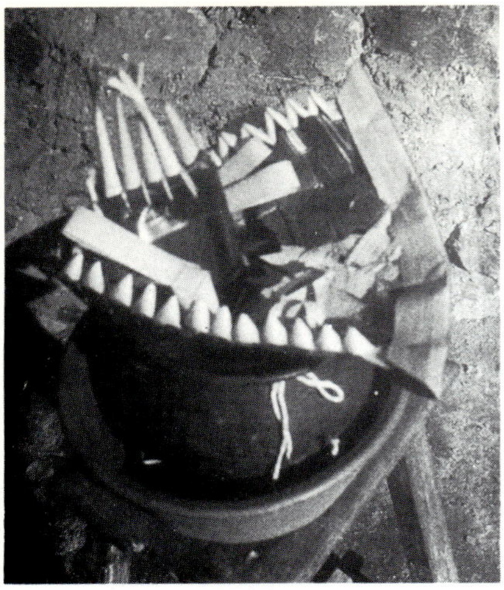

d 1

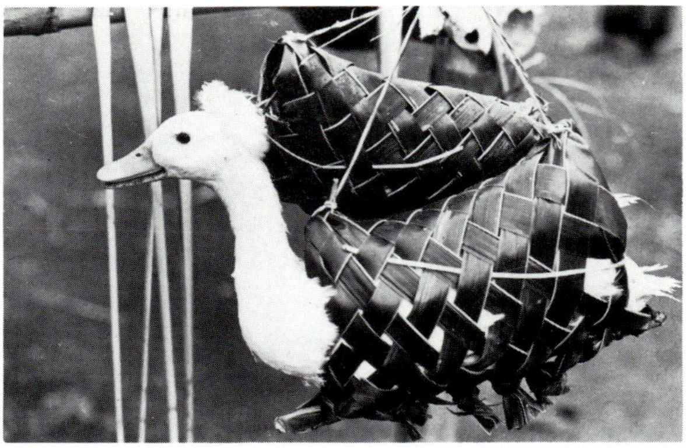

d 2

Zodiac-beaker

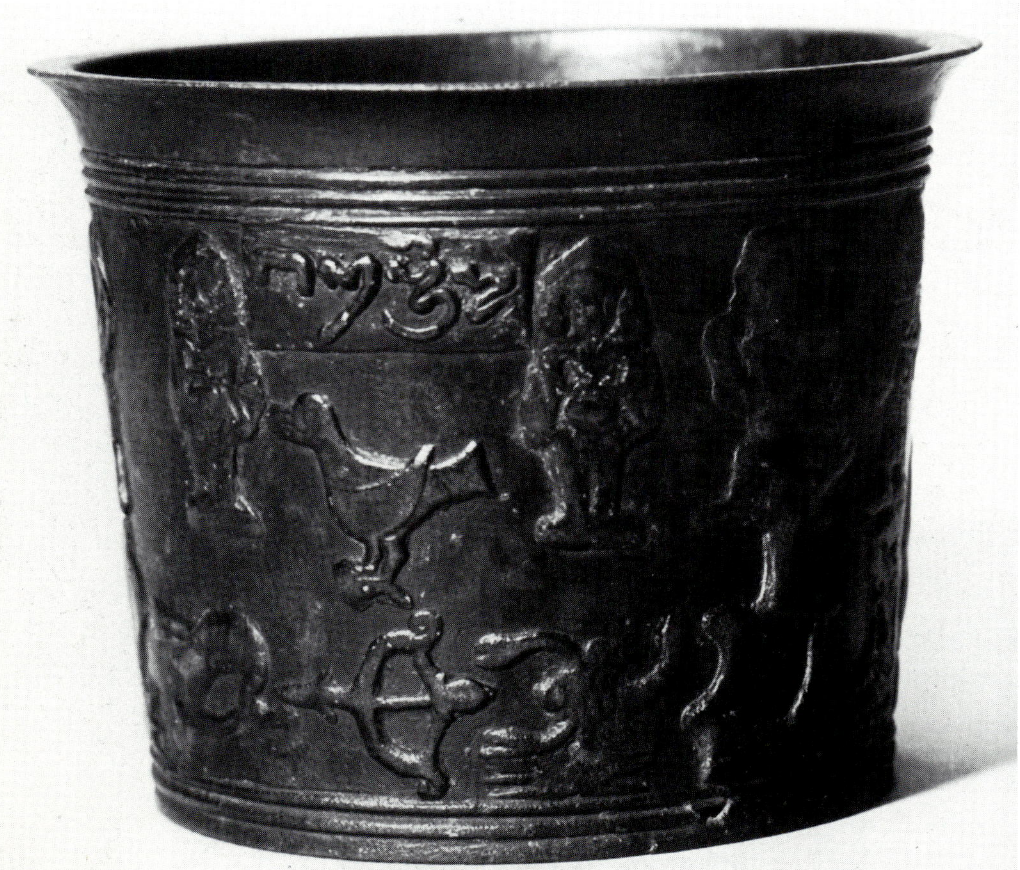

d 3

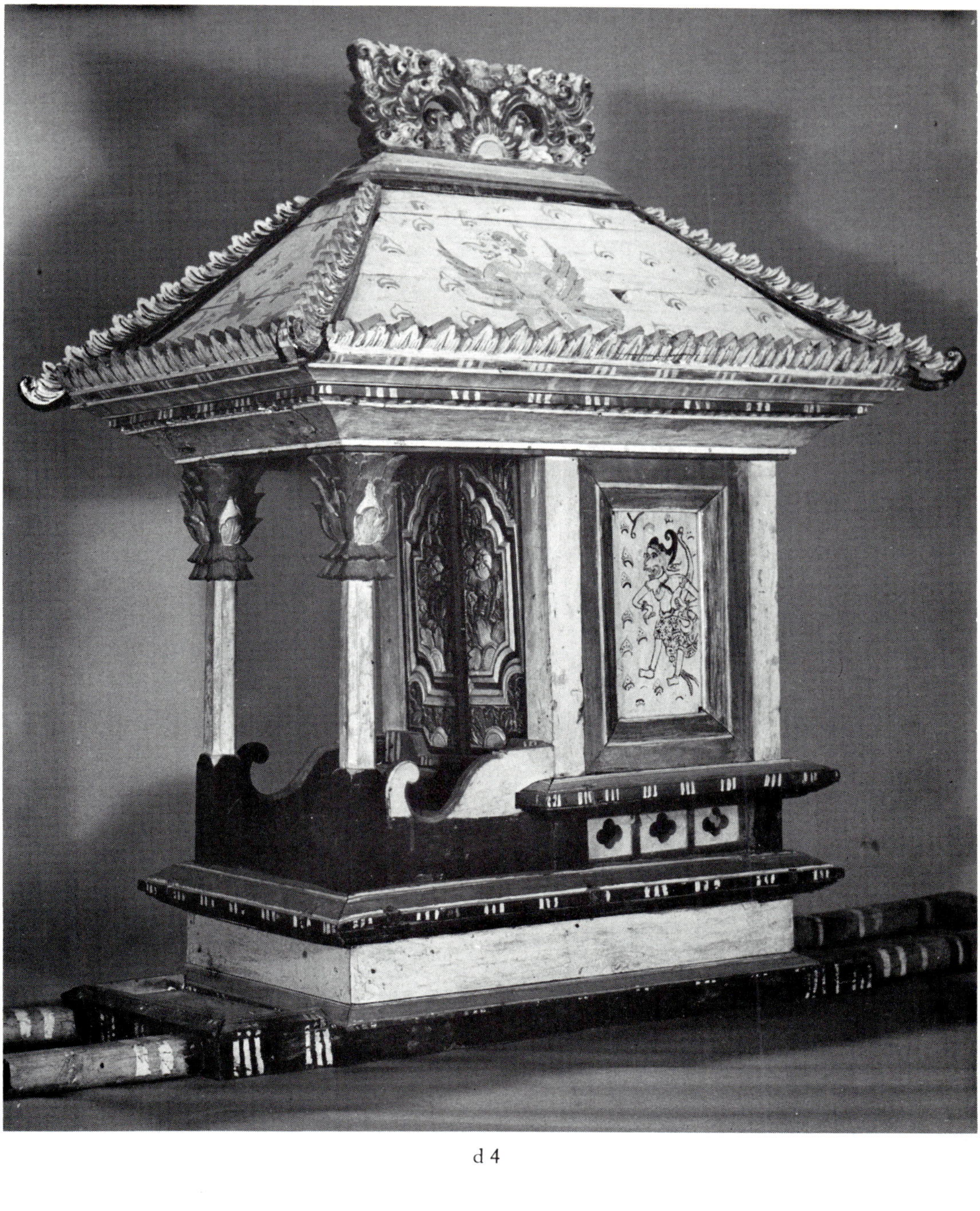

d 4

Yama-Raja, judge in the hereafter, powerful in black magic

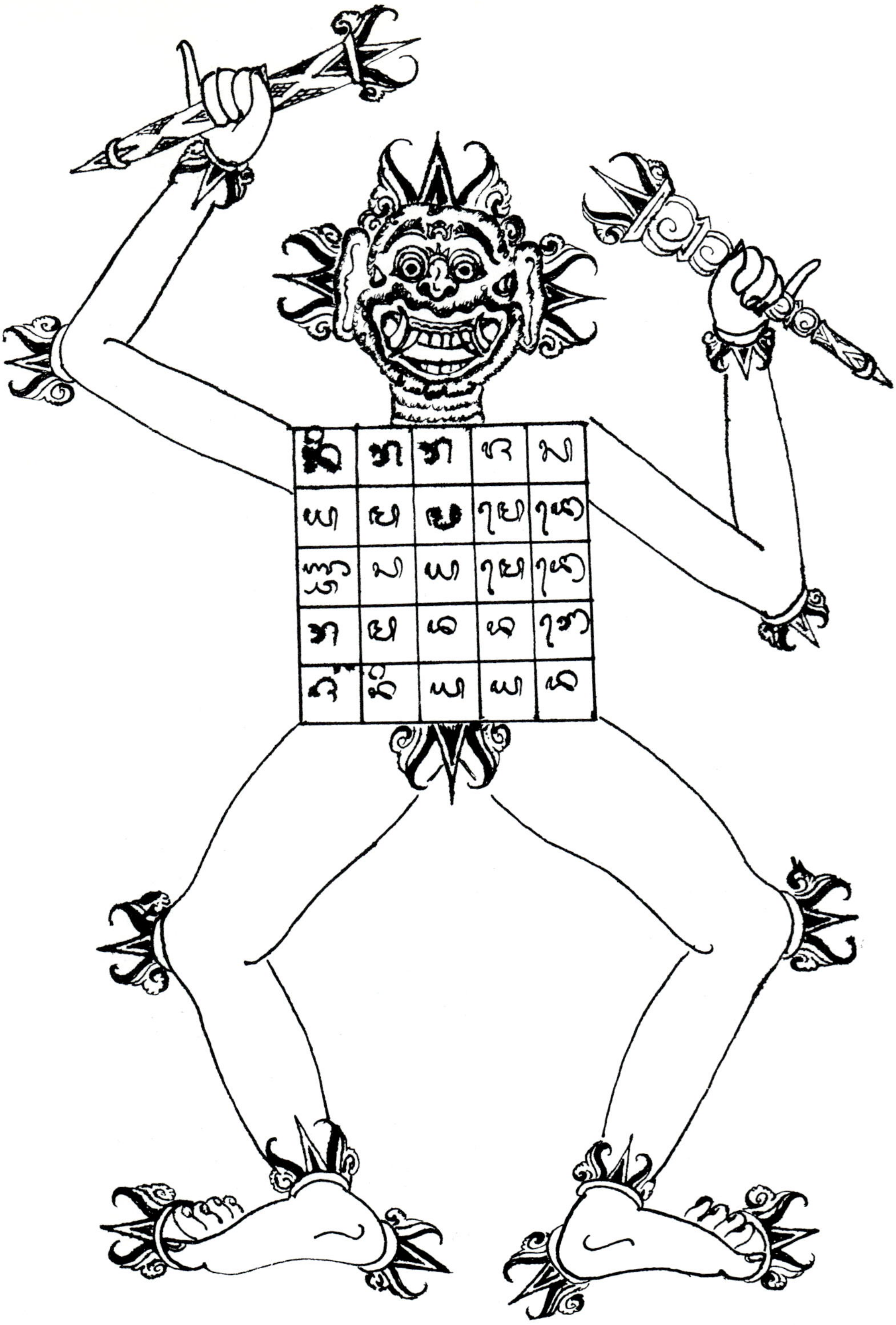

e 1

Drawing from Bodha Kling, Karang Asĕm, North

Yama-Raja, judge in the hereafter, powerful in black magic

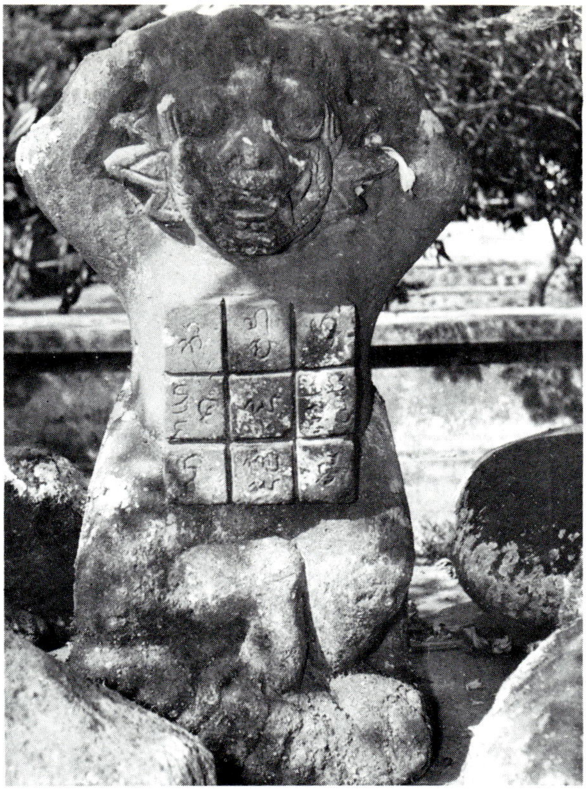

e 2

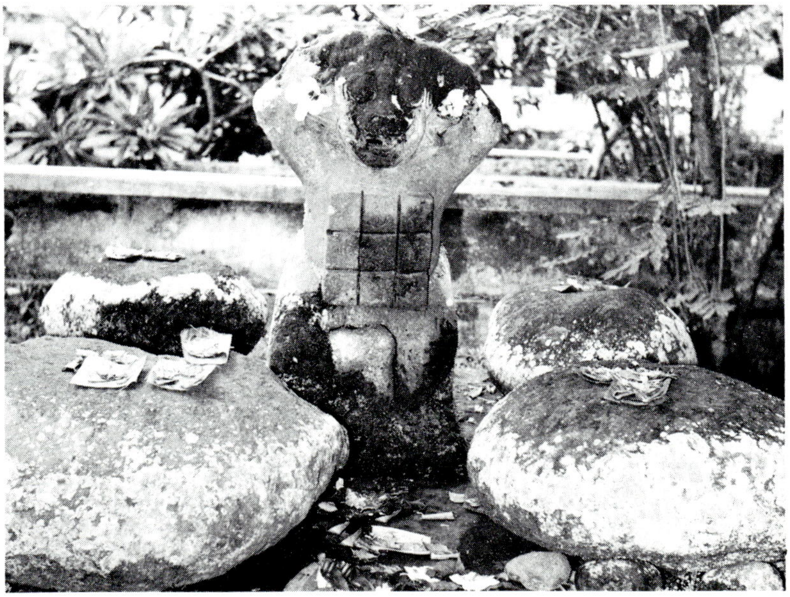

e 3

Sculpture from Kaba-kaba, Tabanan, South

Demon, topsy-turvy

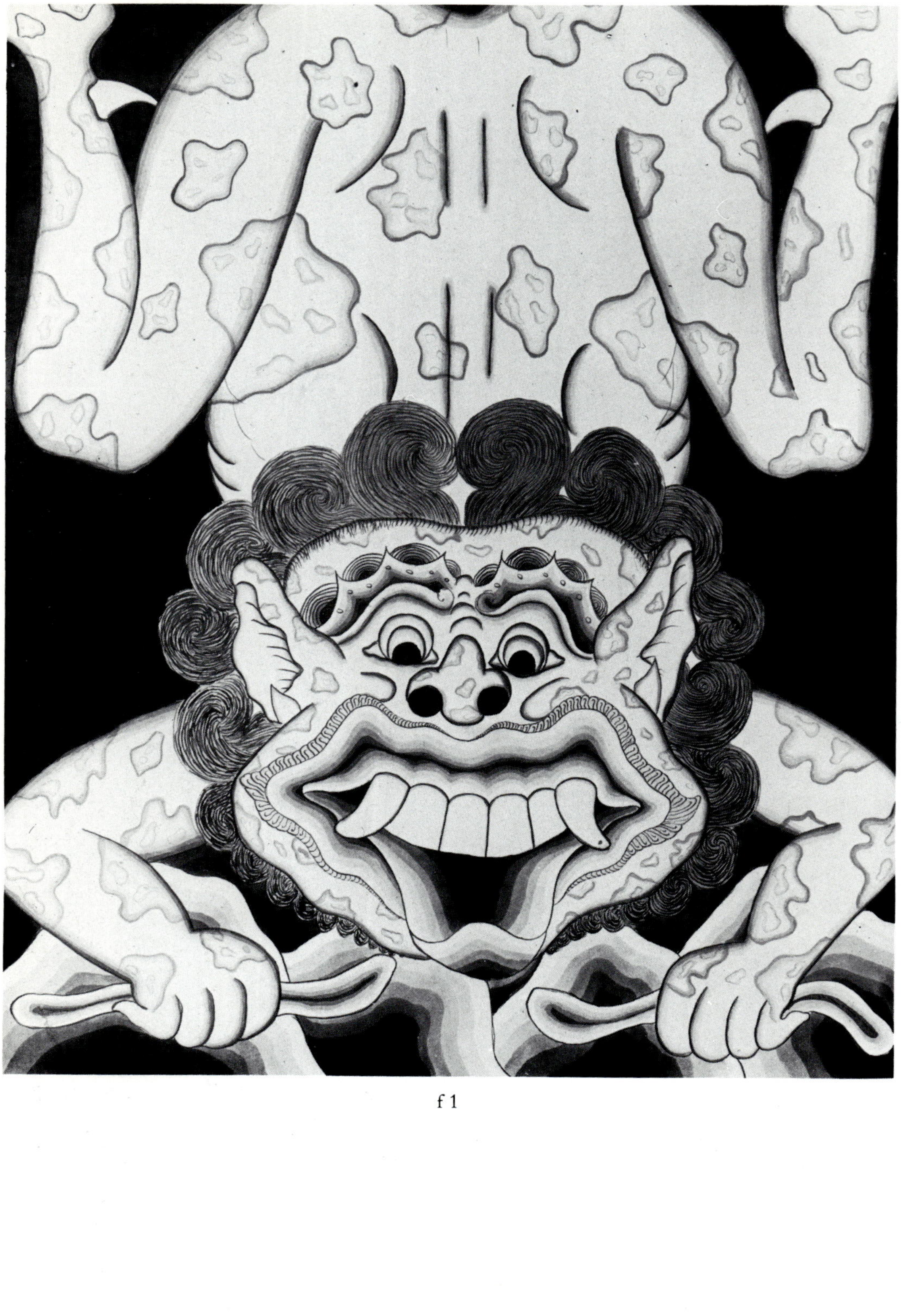

f 1

Bad witch Chalon Arang

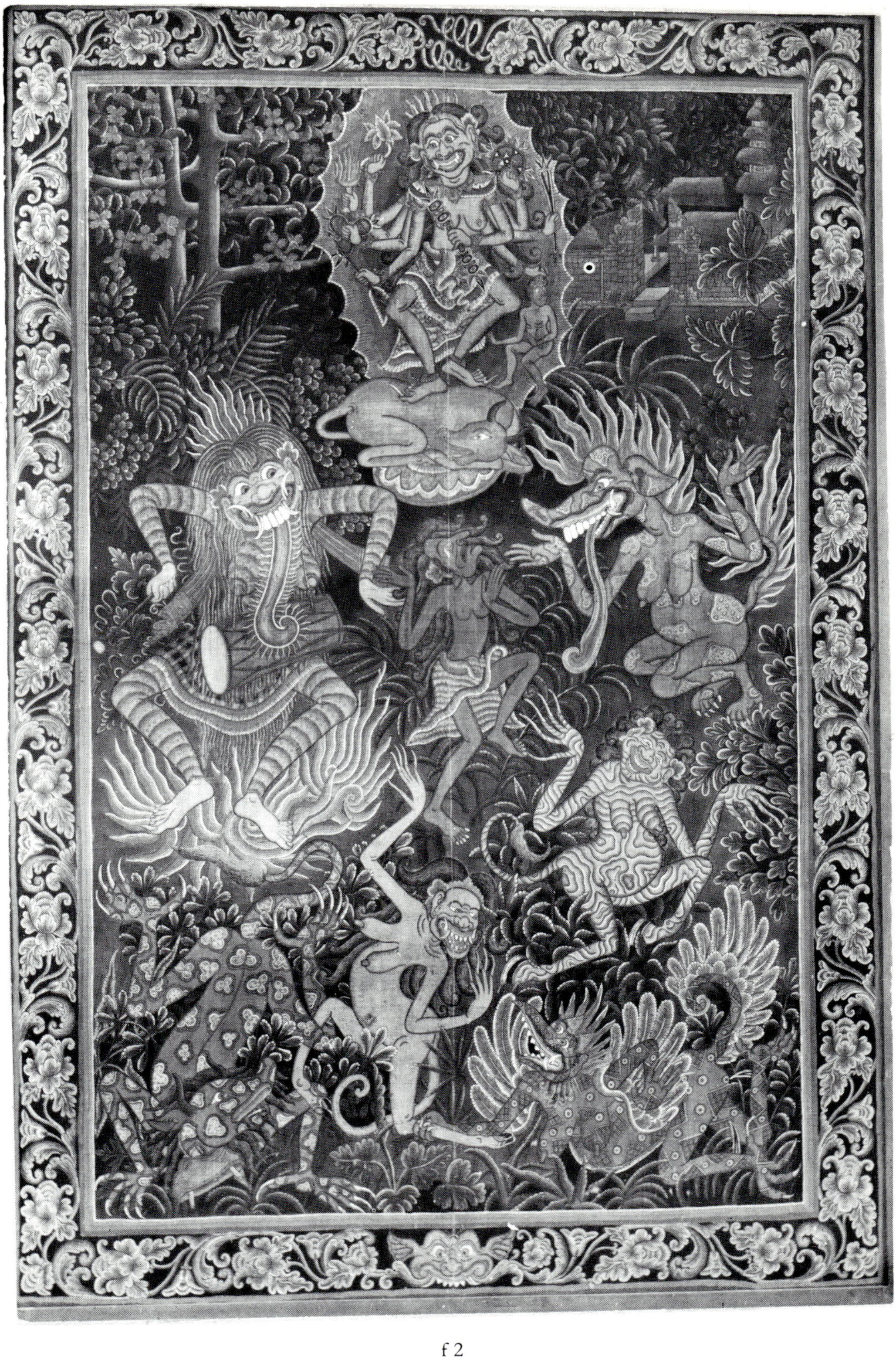

f 2

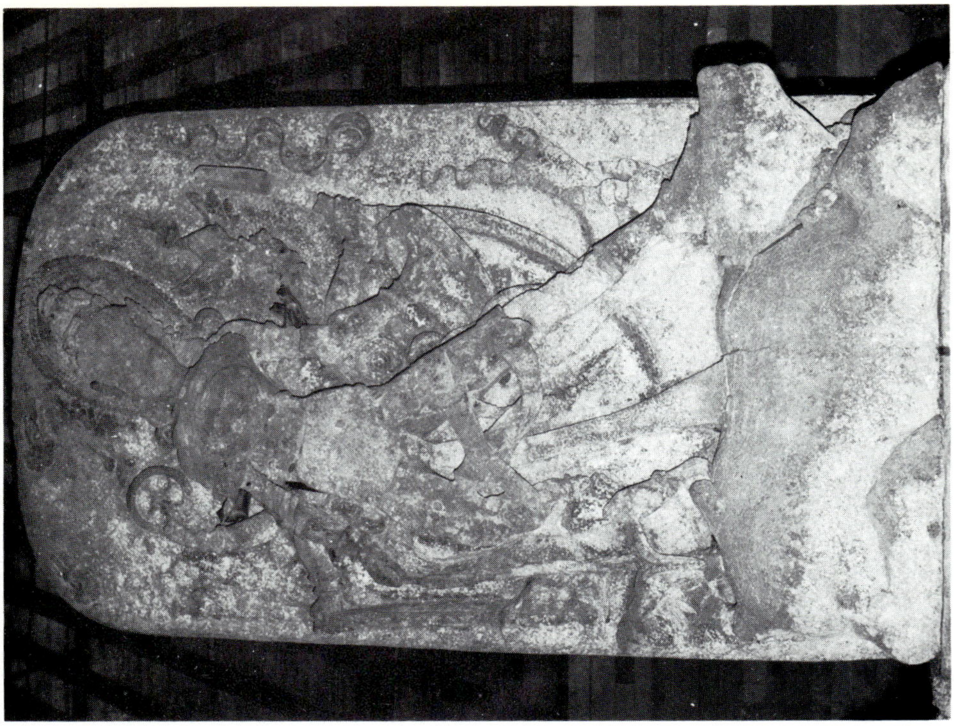

g 2

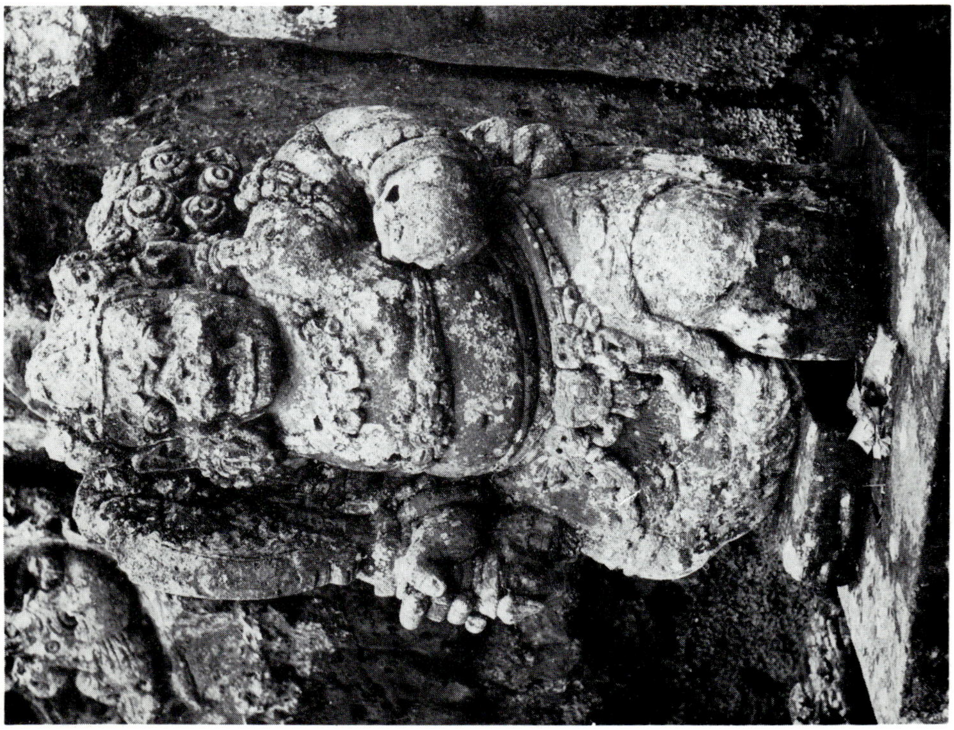

g 1

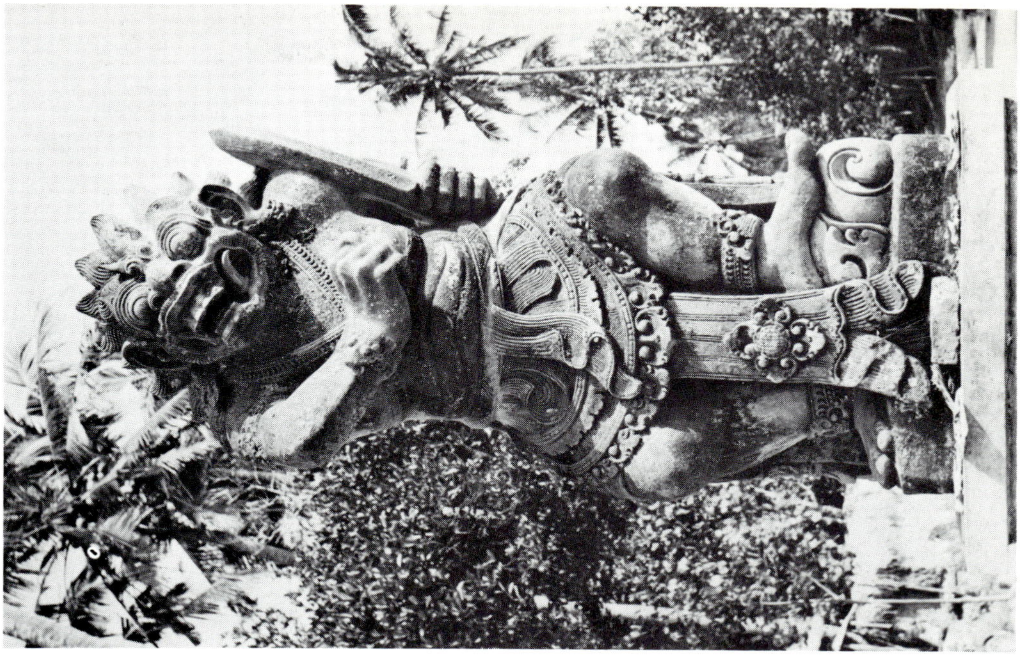

g 4

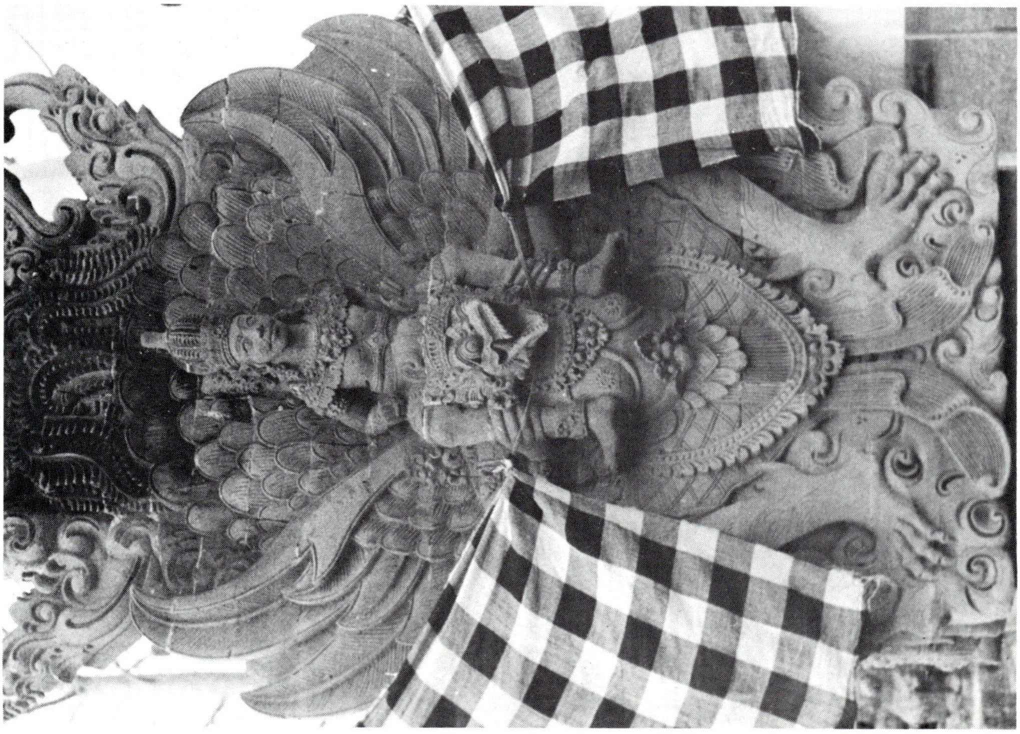

g 3

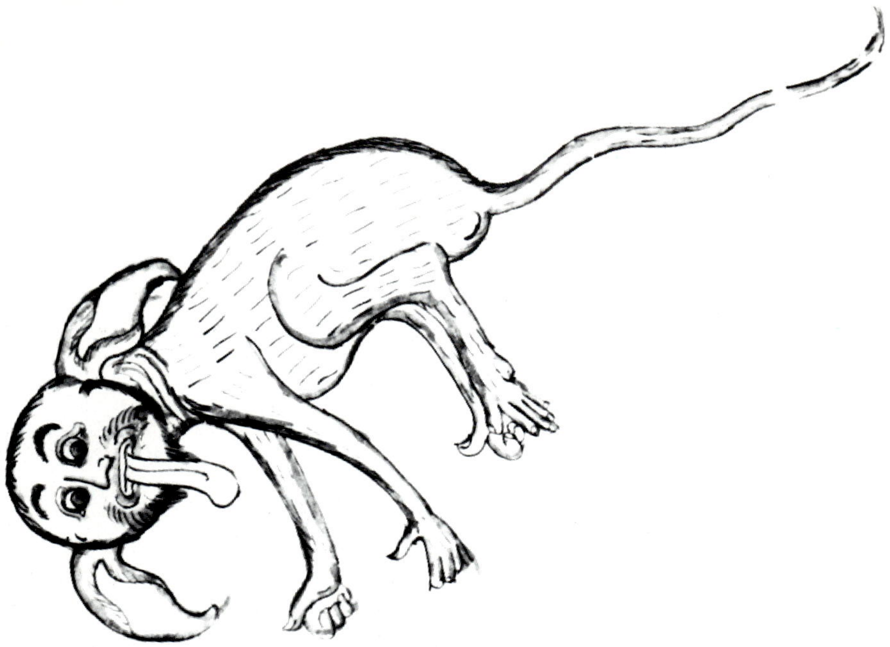

h 2

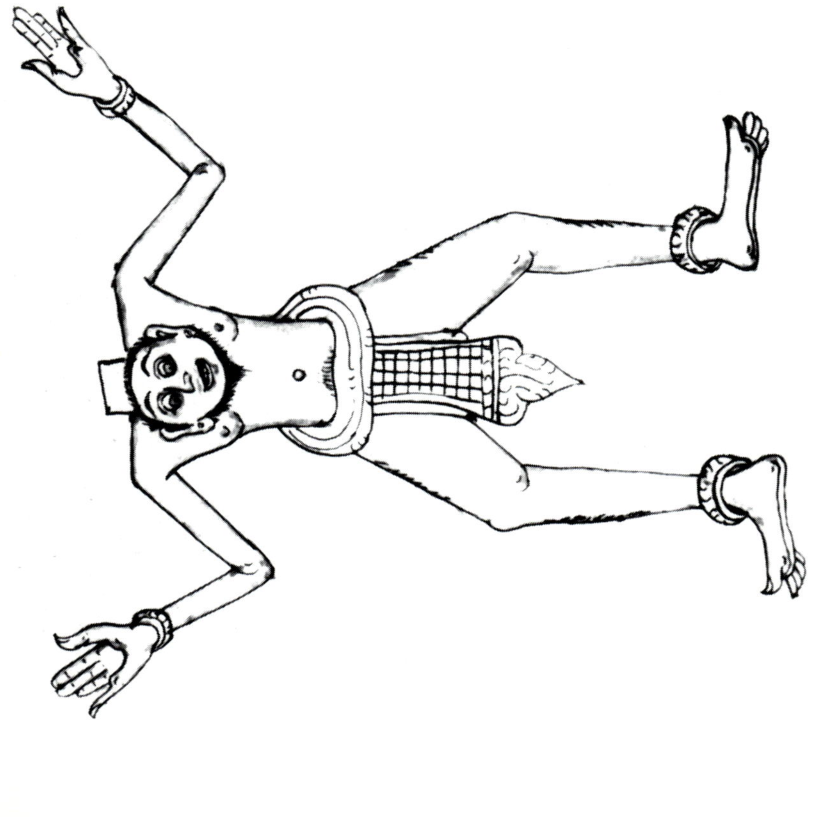

h 1

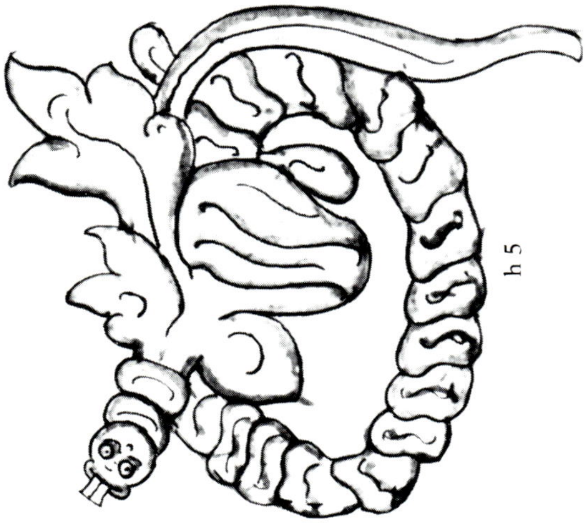

h 5

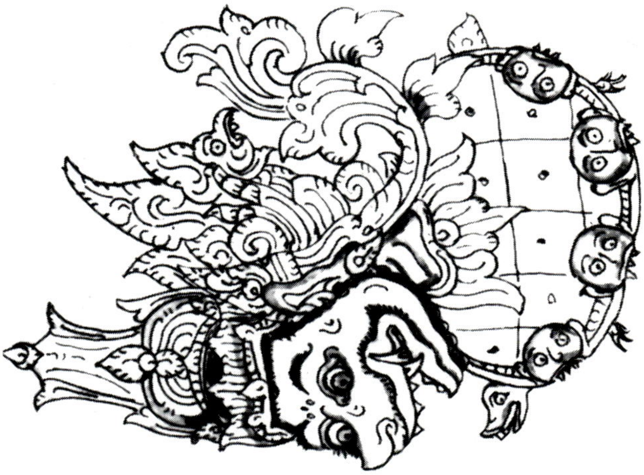

h 6

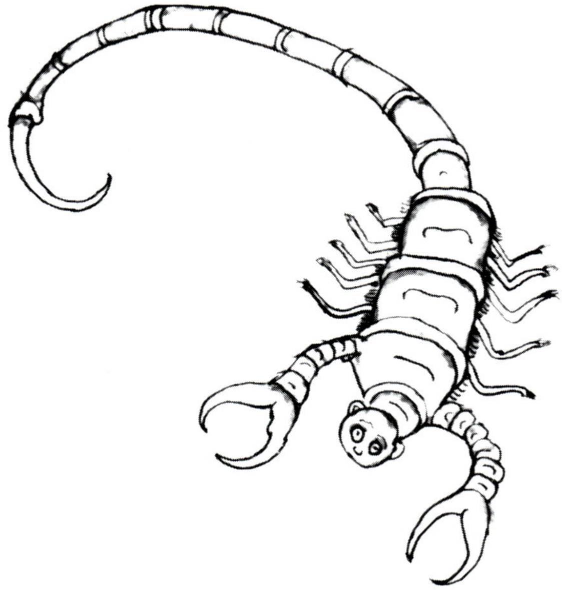

h 3

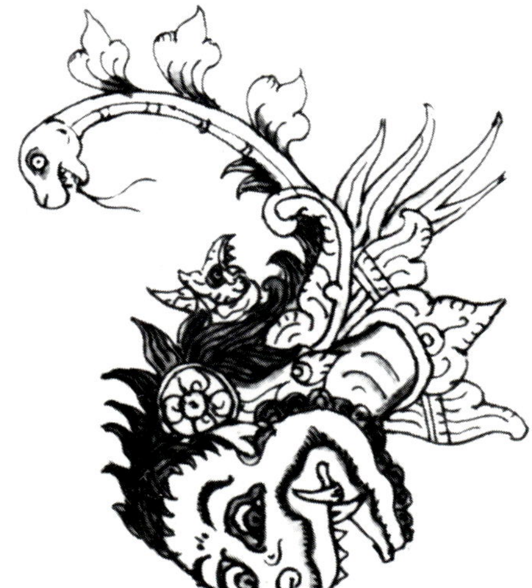

h 4

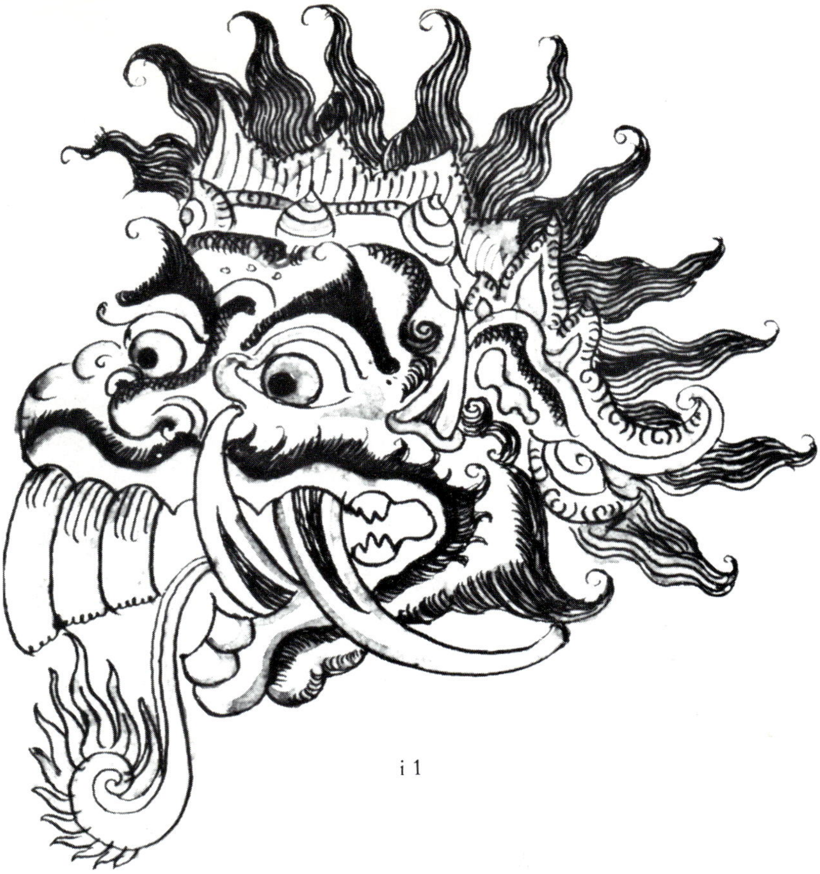

i 1

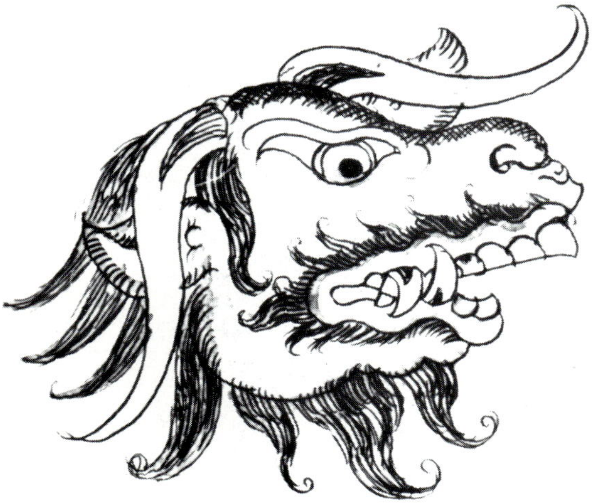

i 2

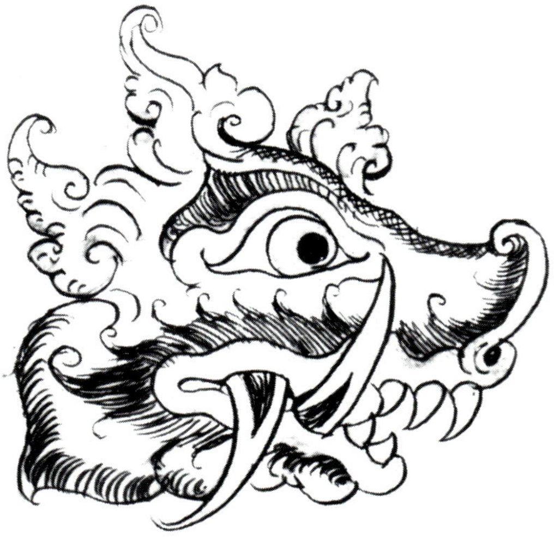

i 3

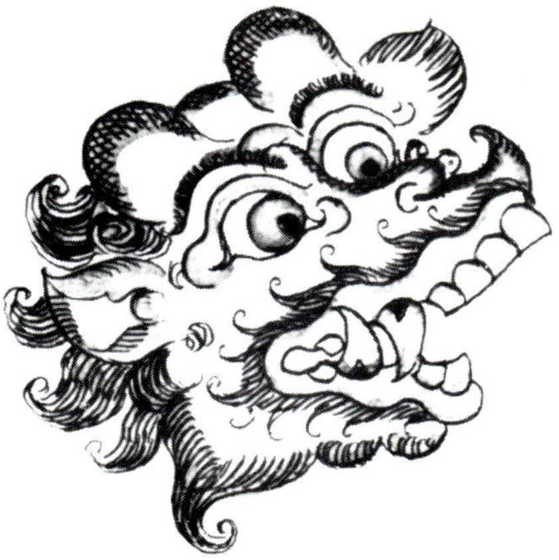

i 4

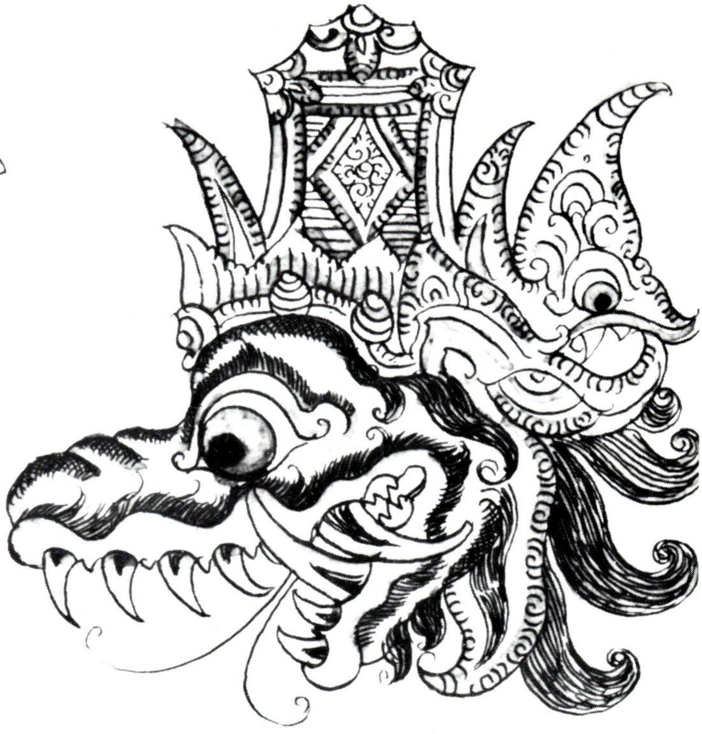

i 5

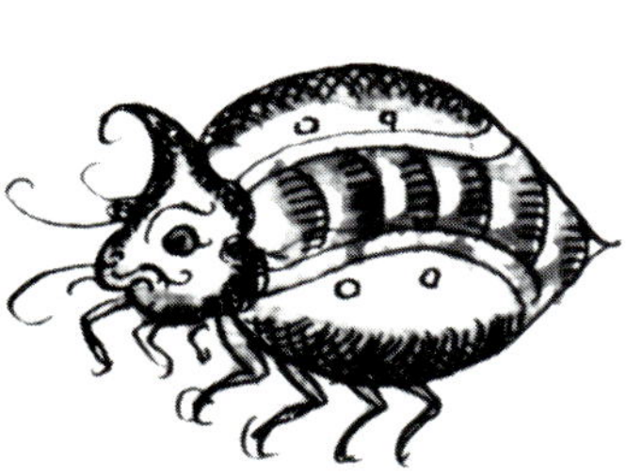

i 6

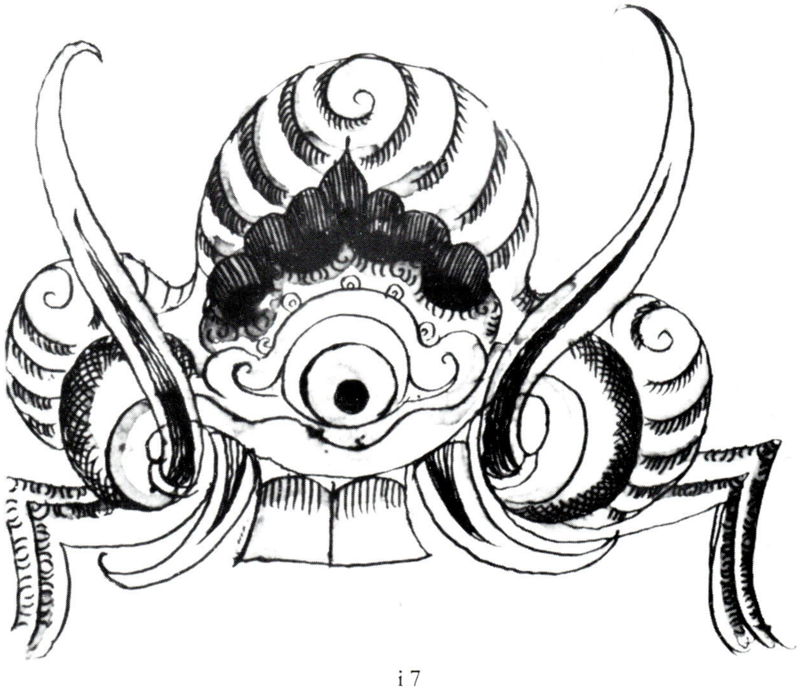

i 7

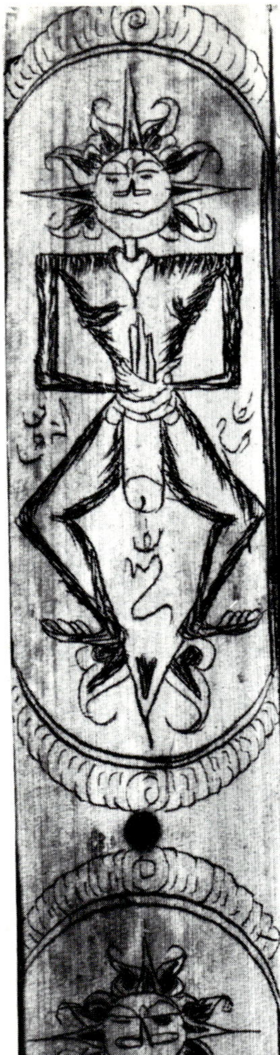

j 1

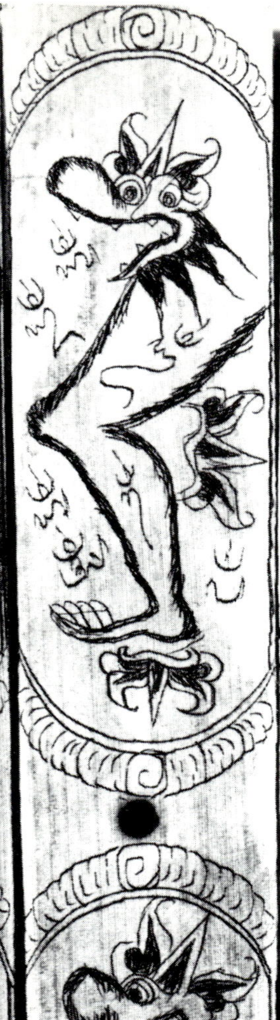

j 2

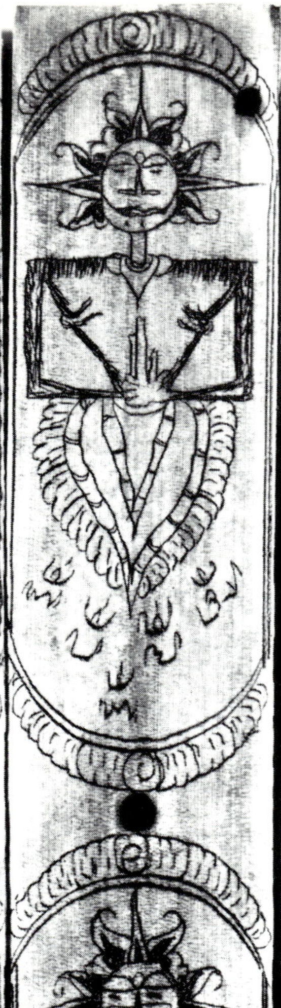

j 3

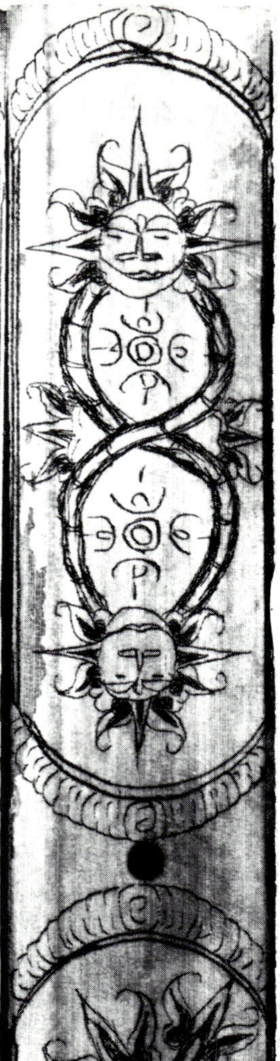

j 4

Counter-magic

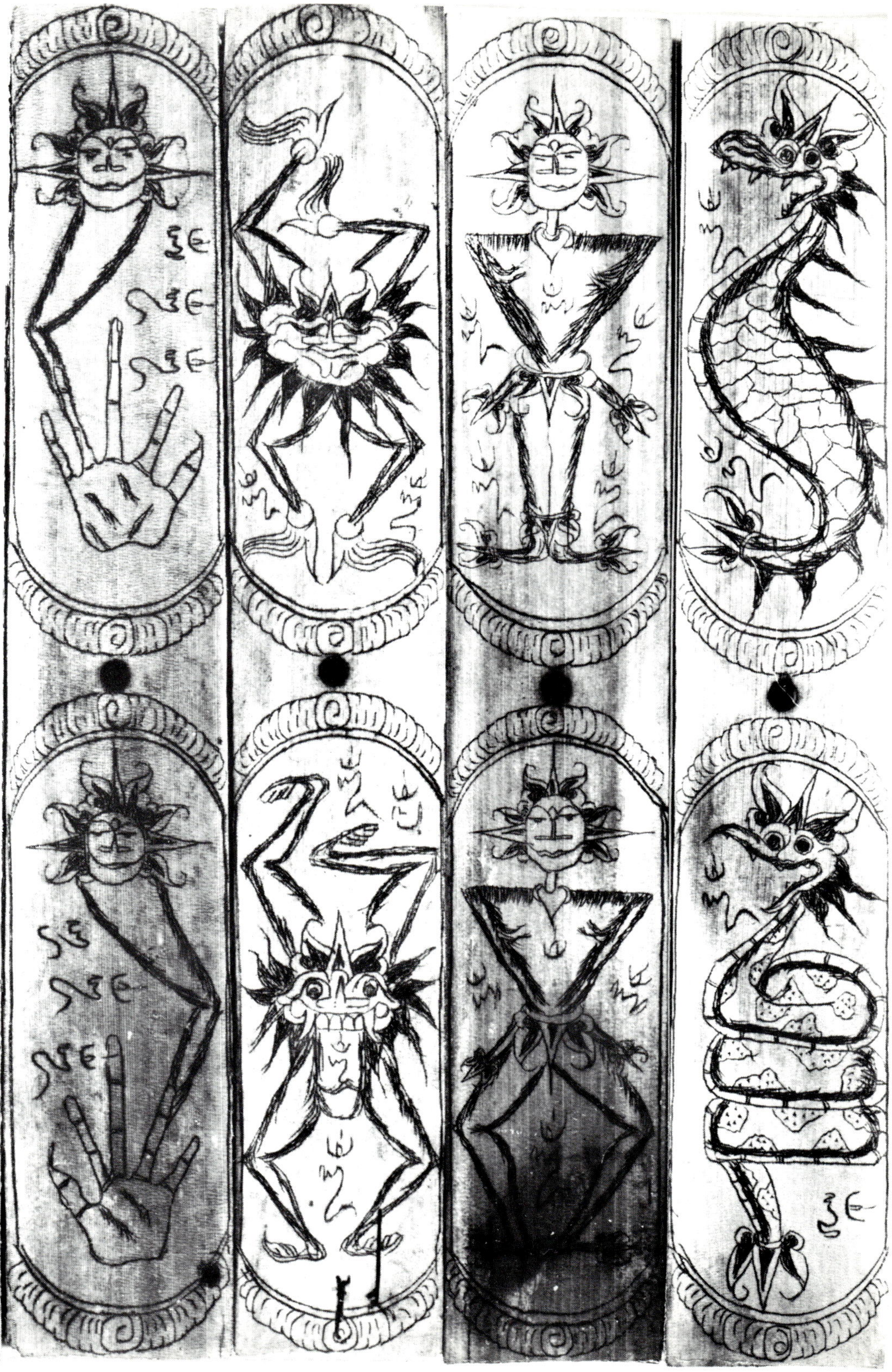

j 5 j 6 j 7 j 8

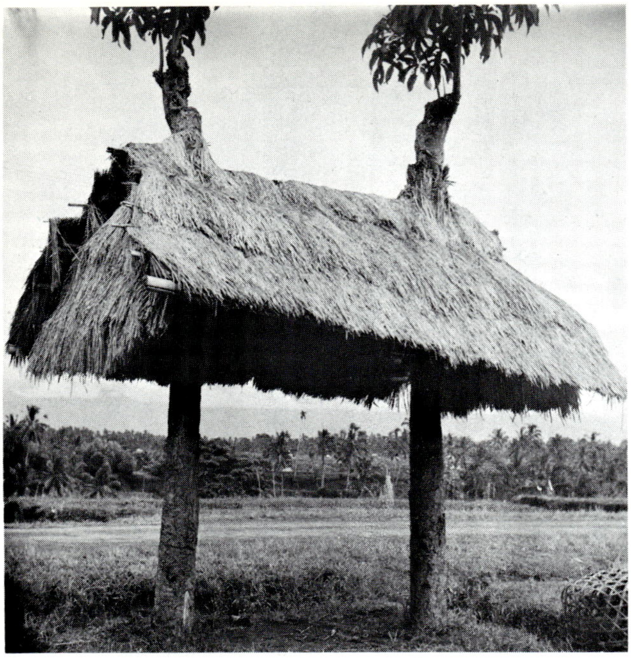

k 5

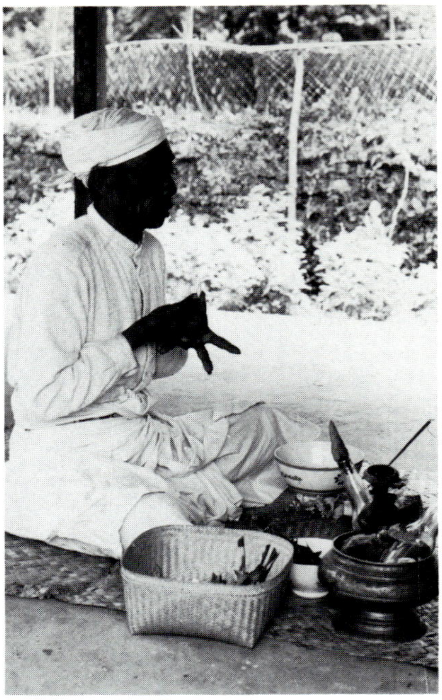

k 1

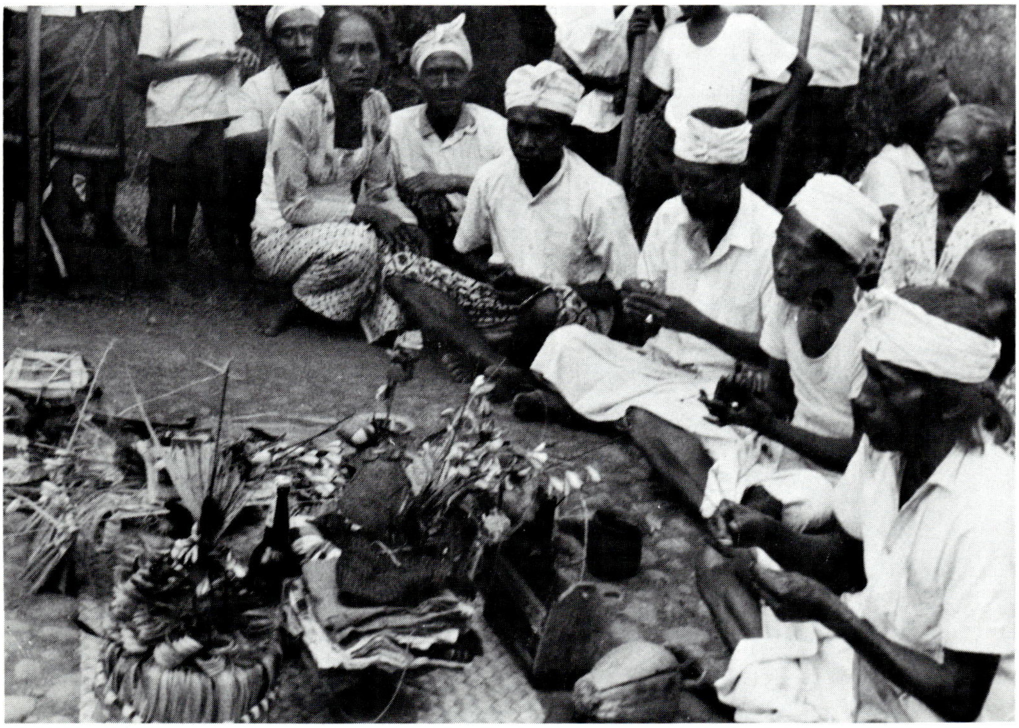

k 2

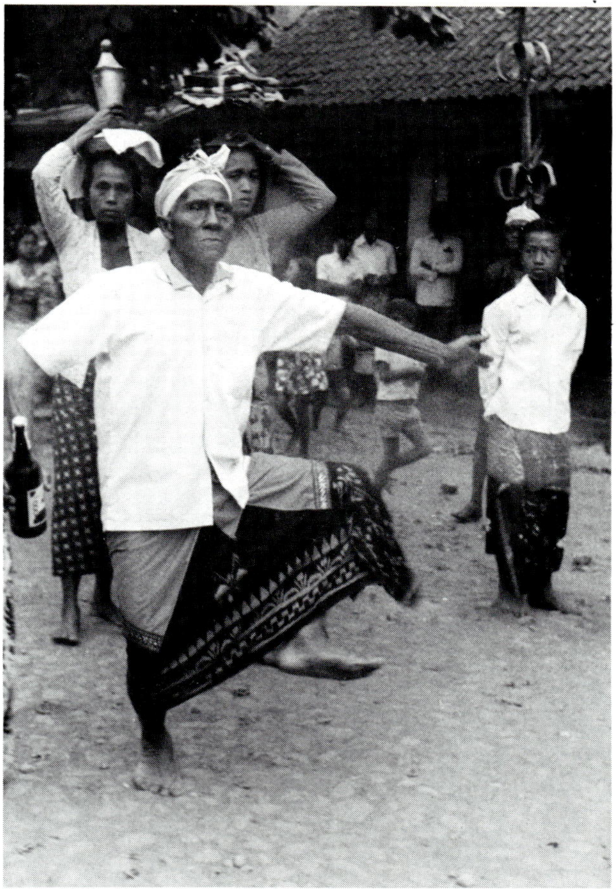

k 3

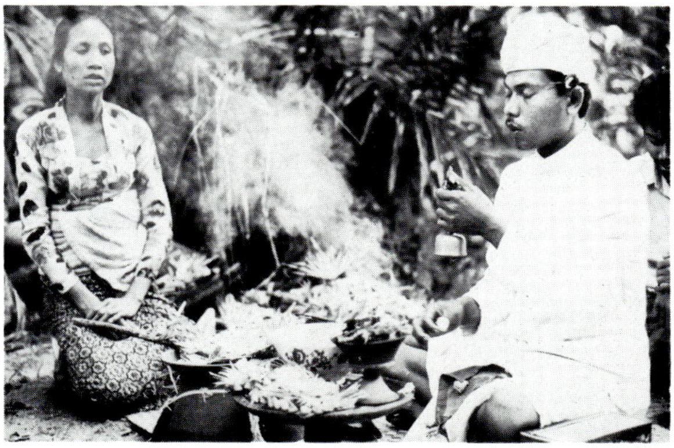

k 4

Brahman priests, husband and wife

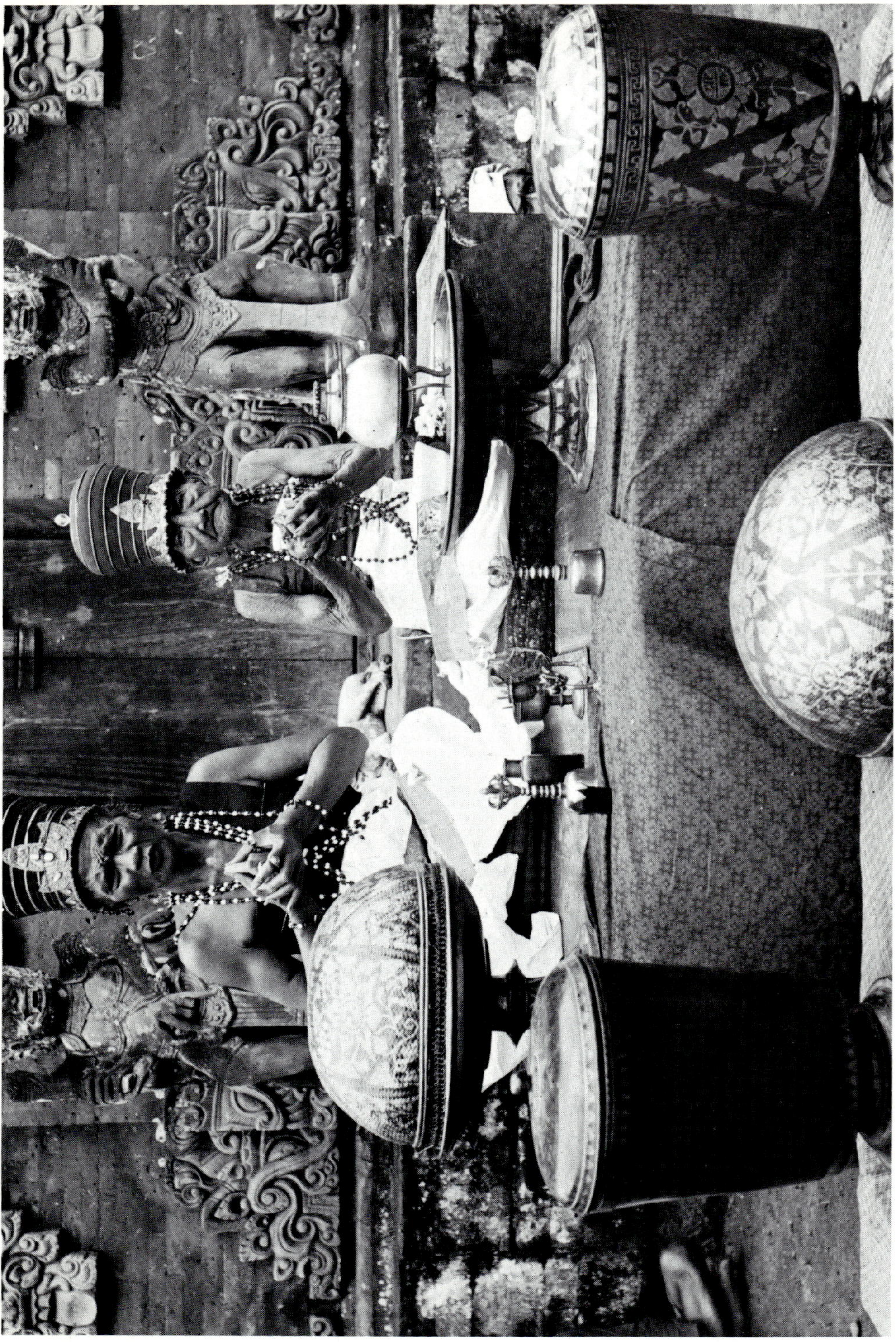

m 1

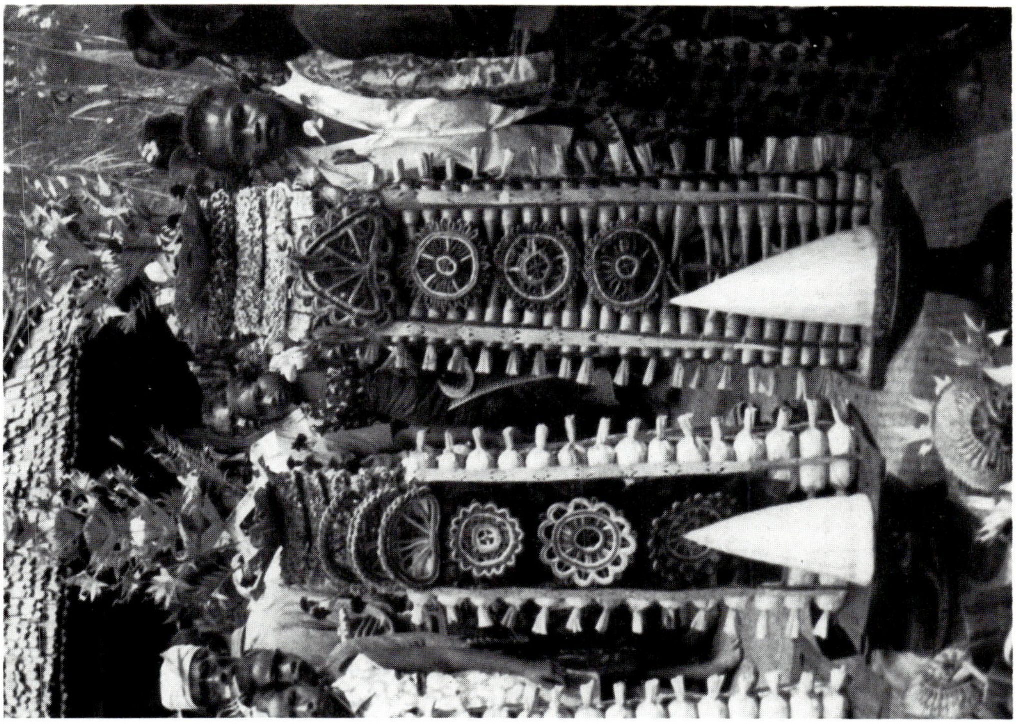

m 3

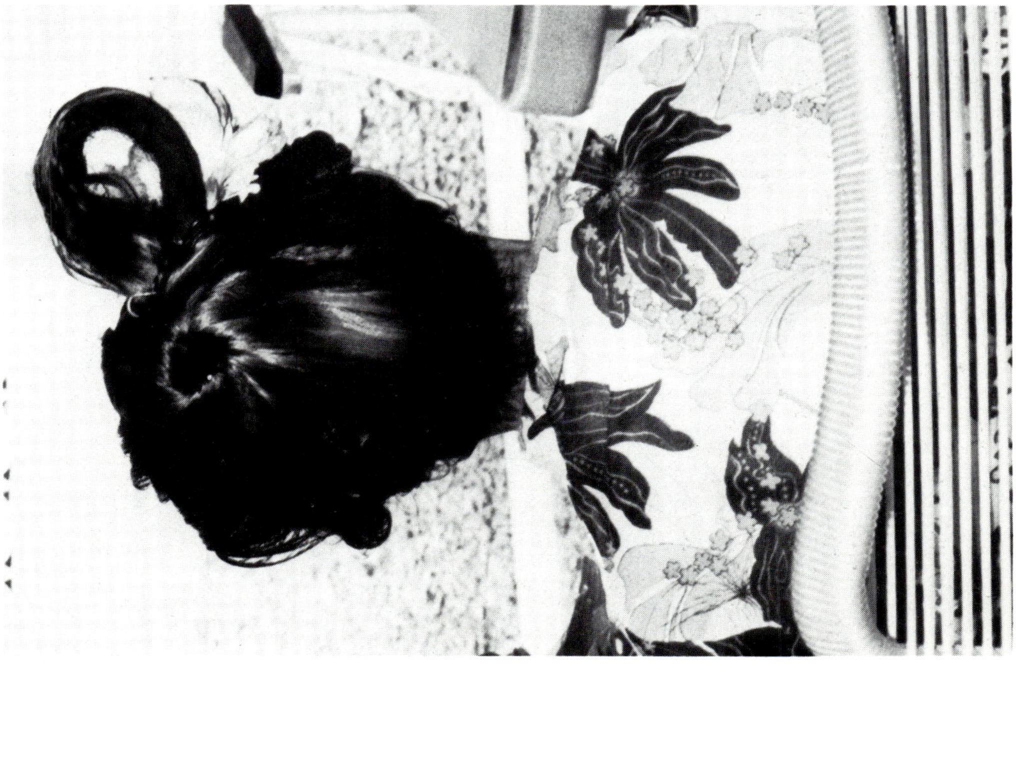

m 2

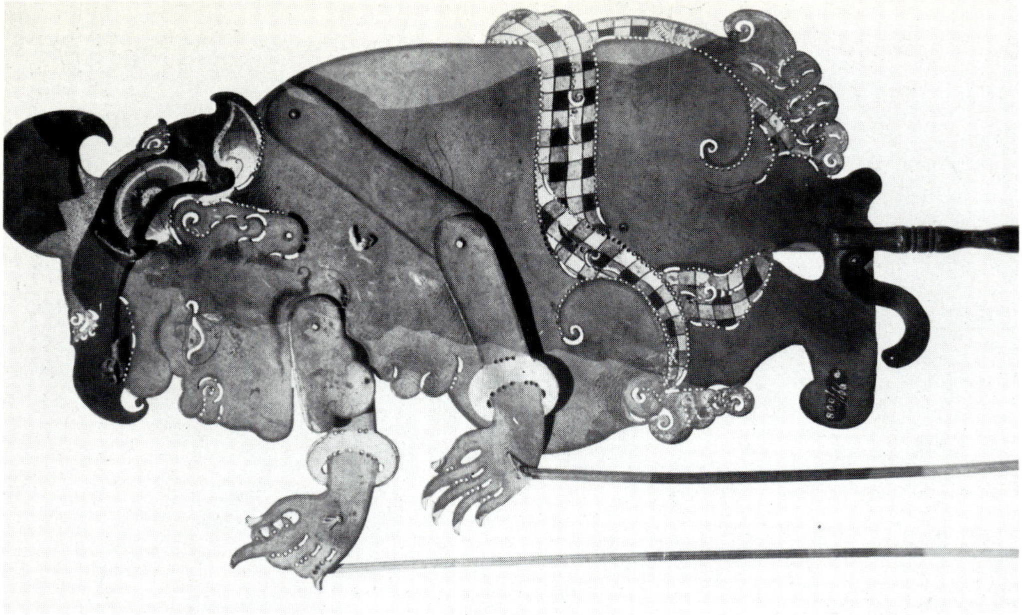

n 3

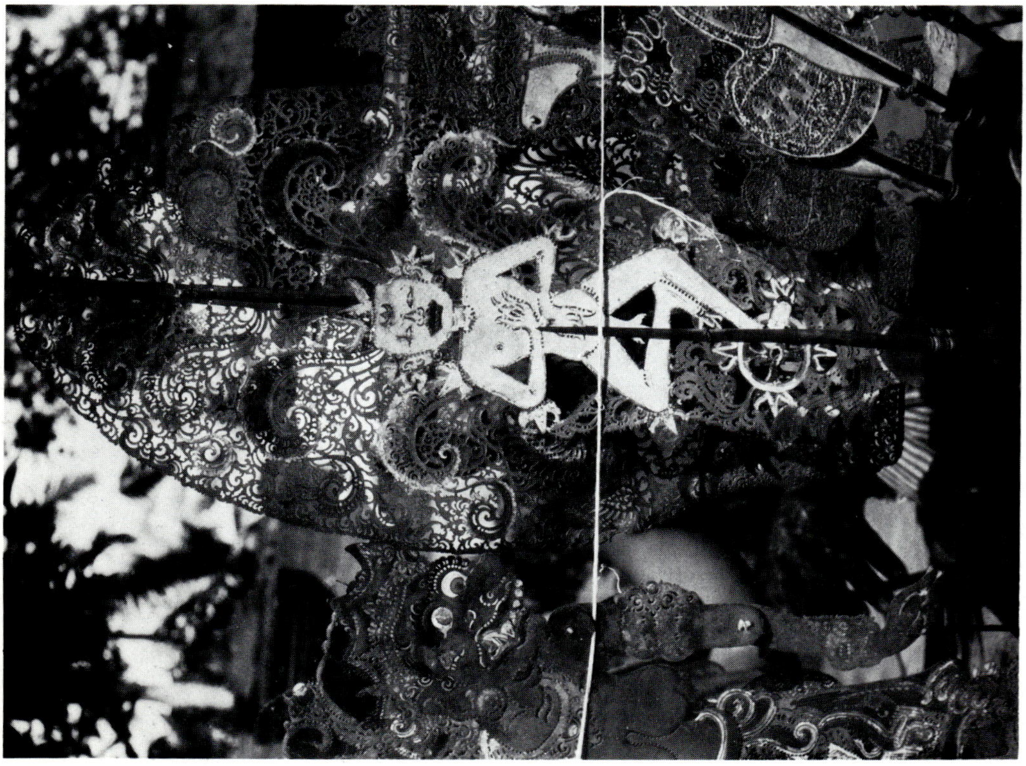

n 1

'Shadow-play' at day-time

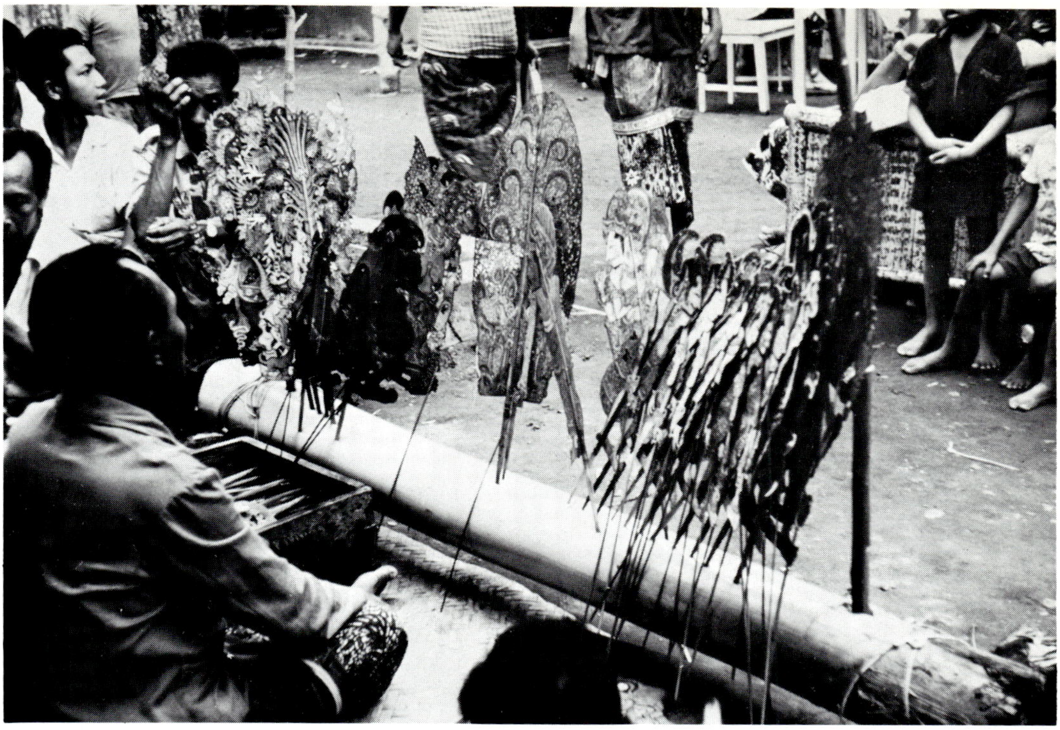

n 2

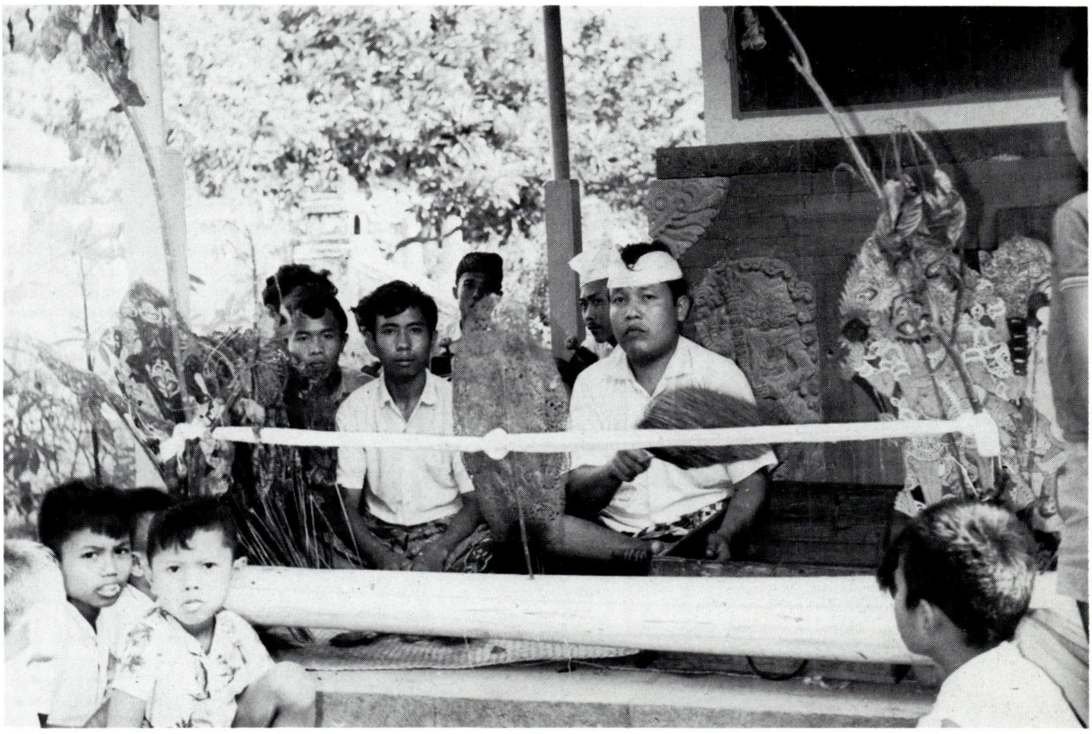

n 4

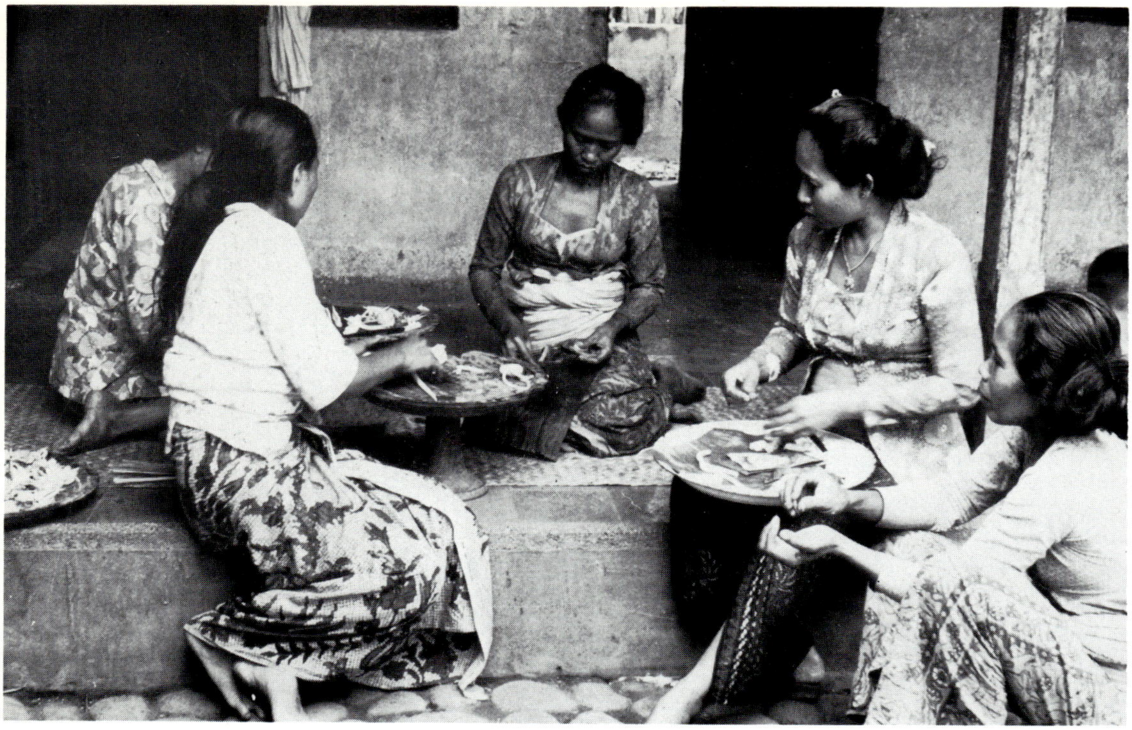

o 1

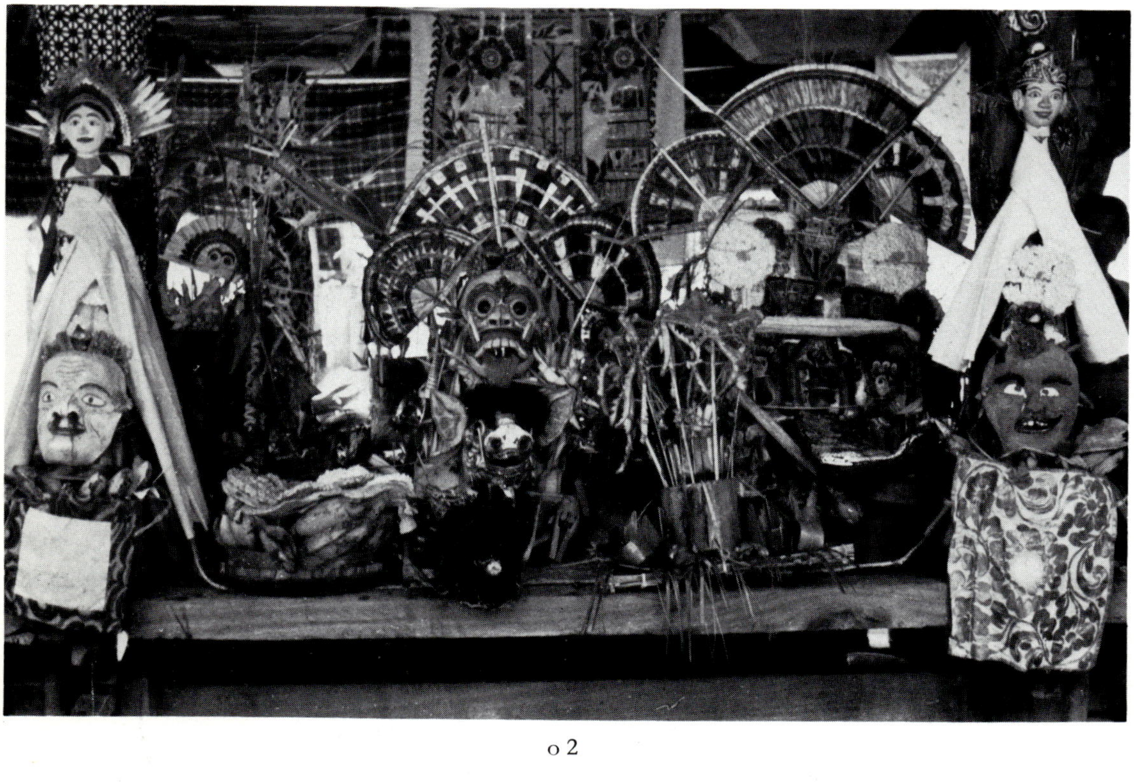

o 2

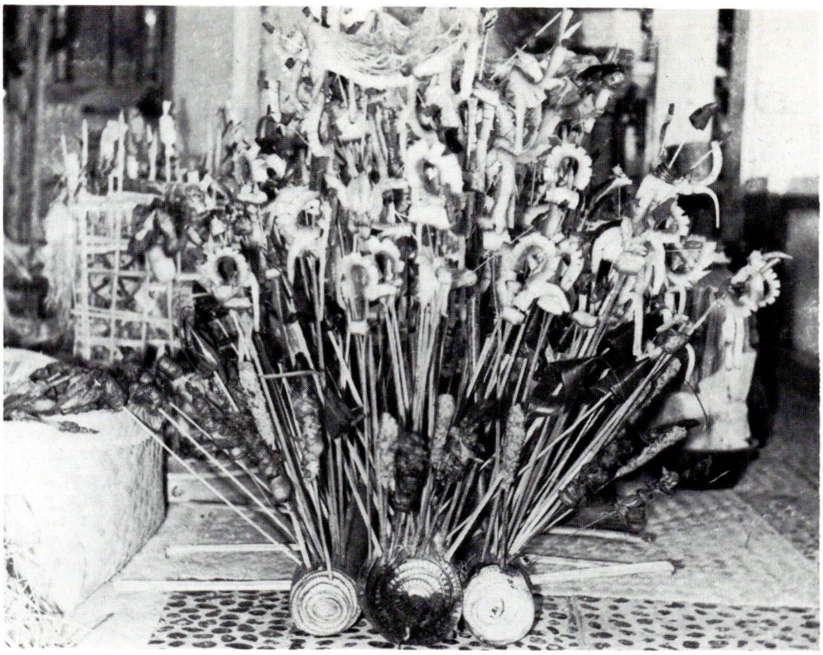

o 3

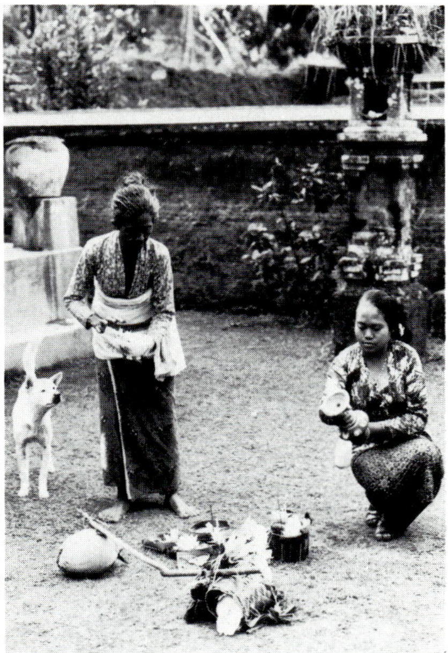

o 4

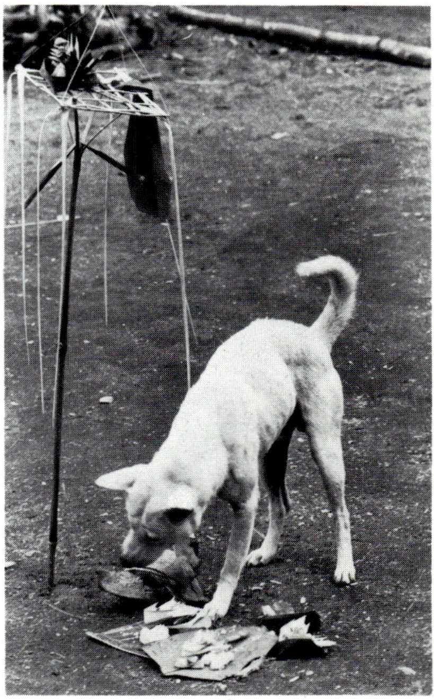

o 5

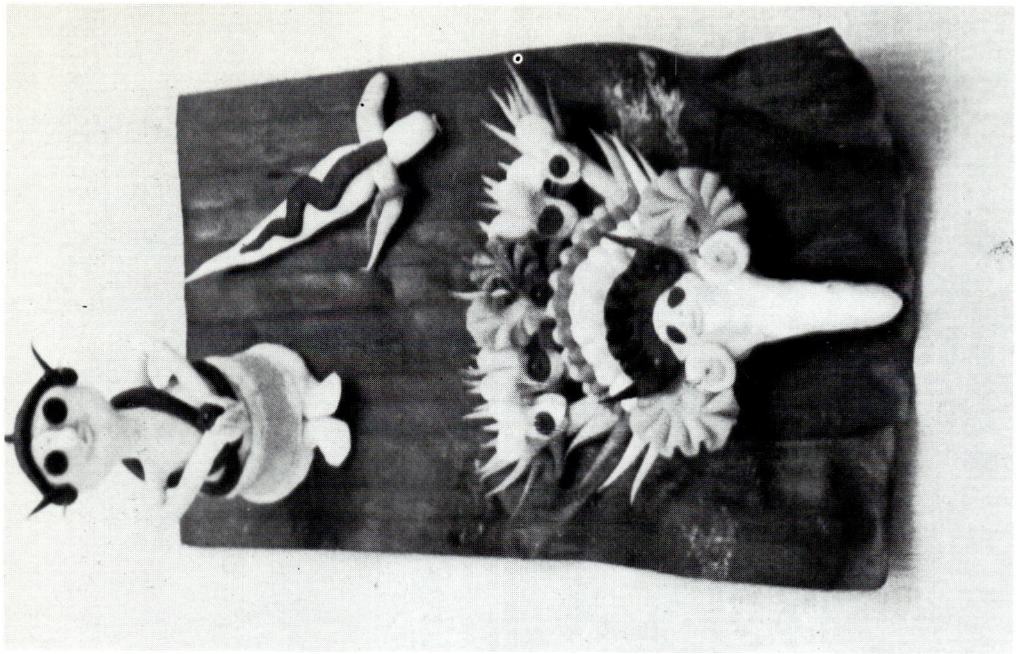

p 2

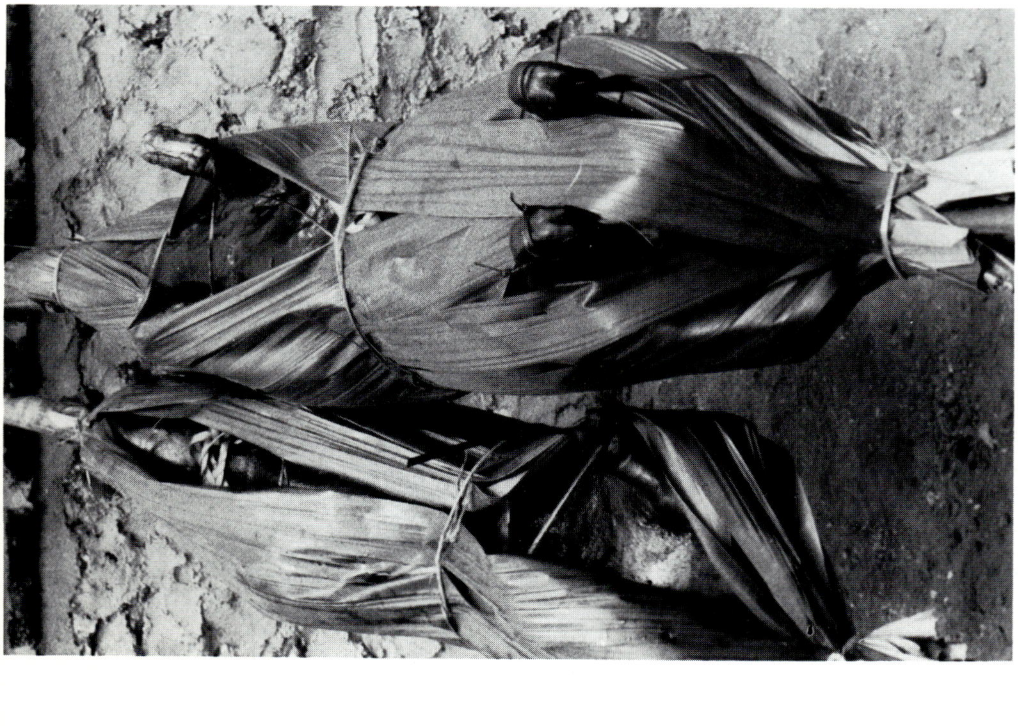

p 1

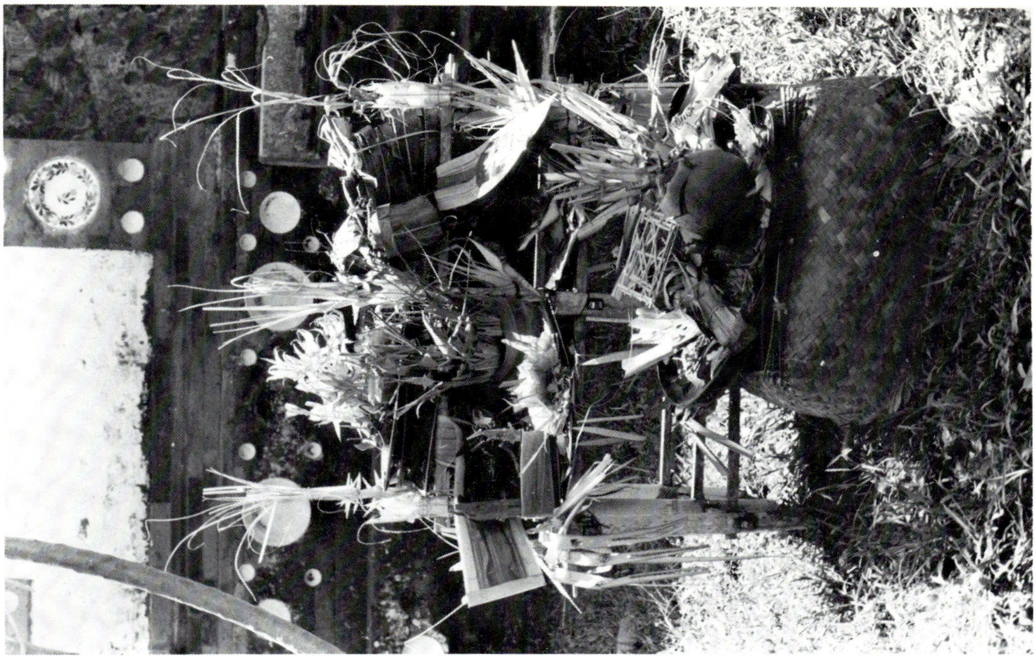

p 4

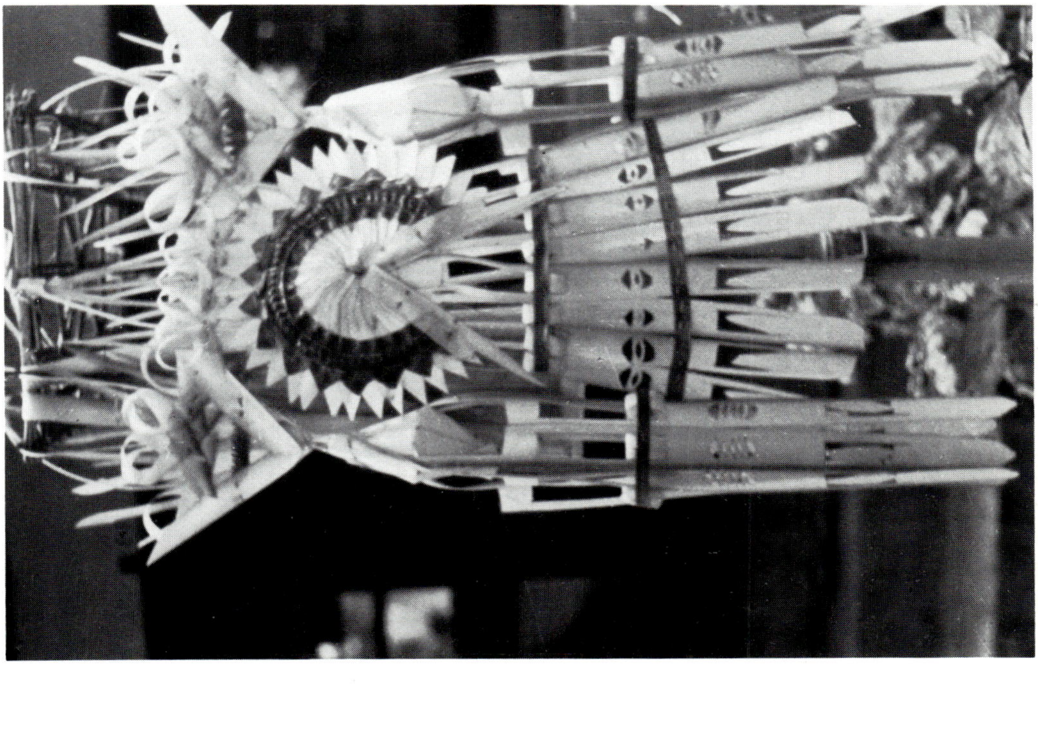

p 3

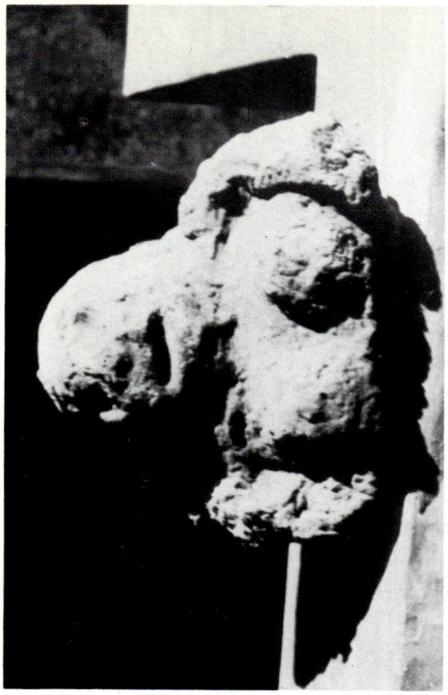

q 2

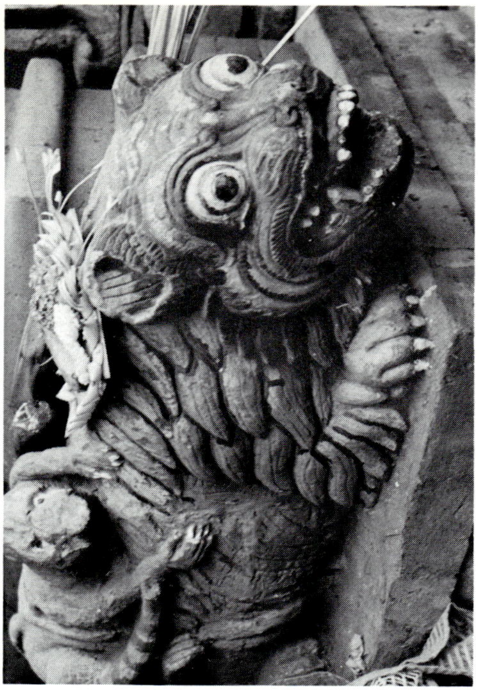

q 3

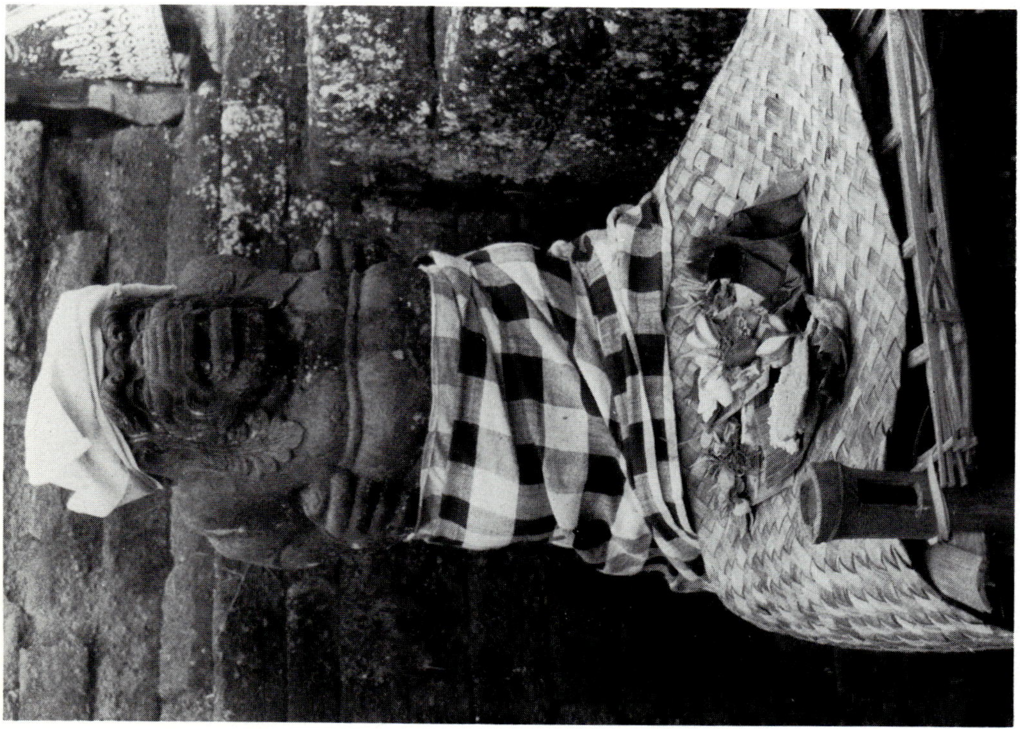

q 1

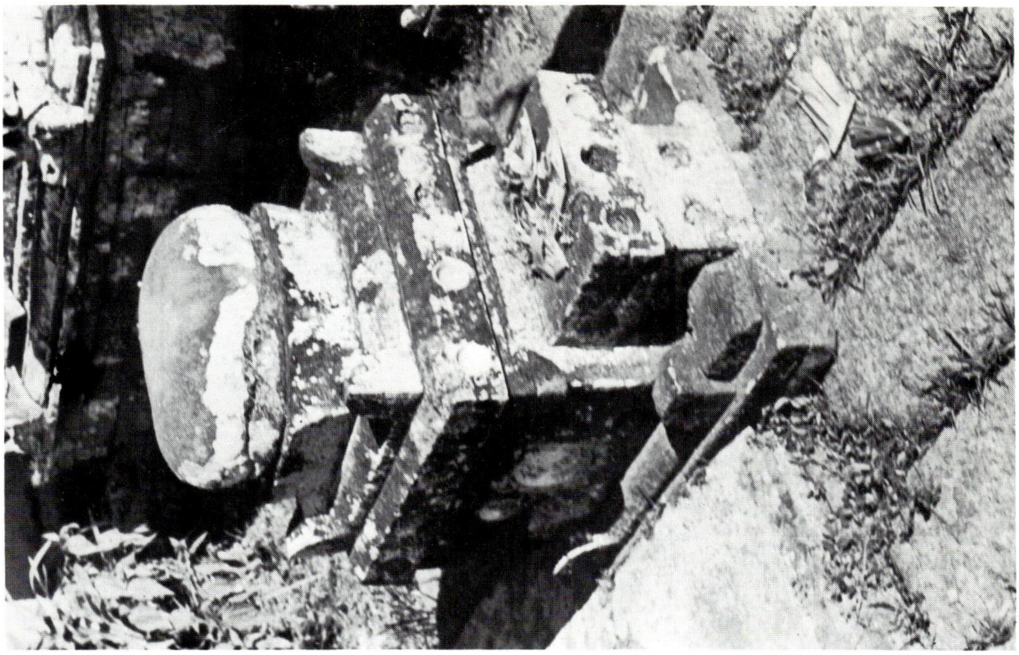

95

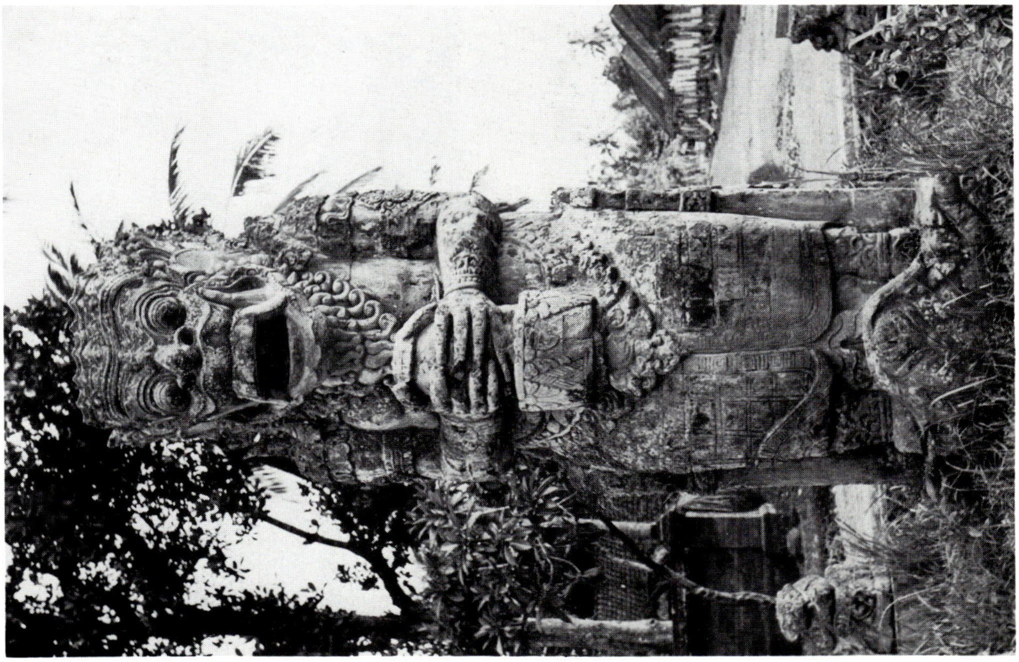

94

Sri and Sadana

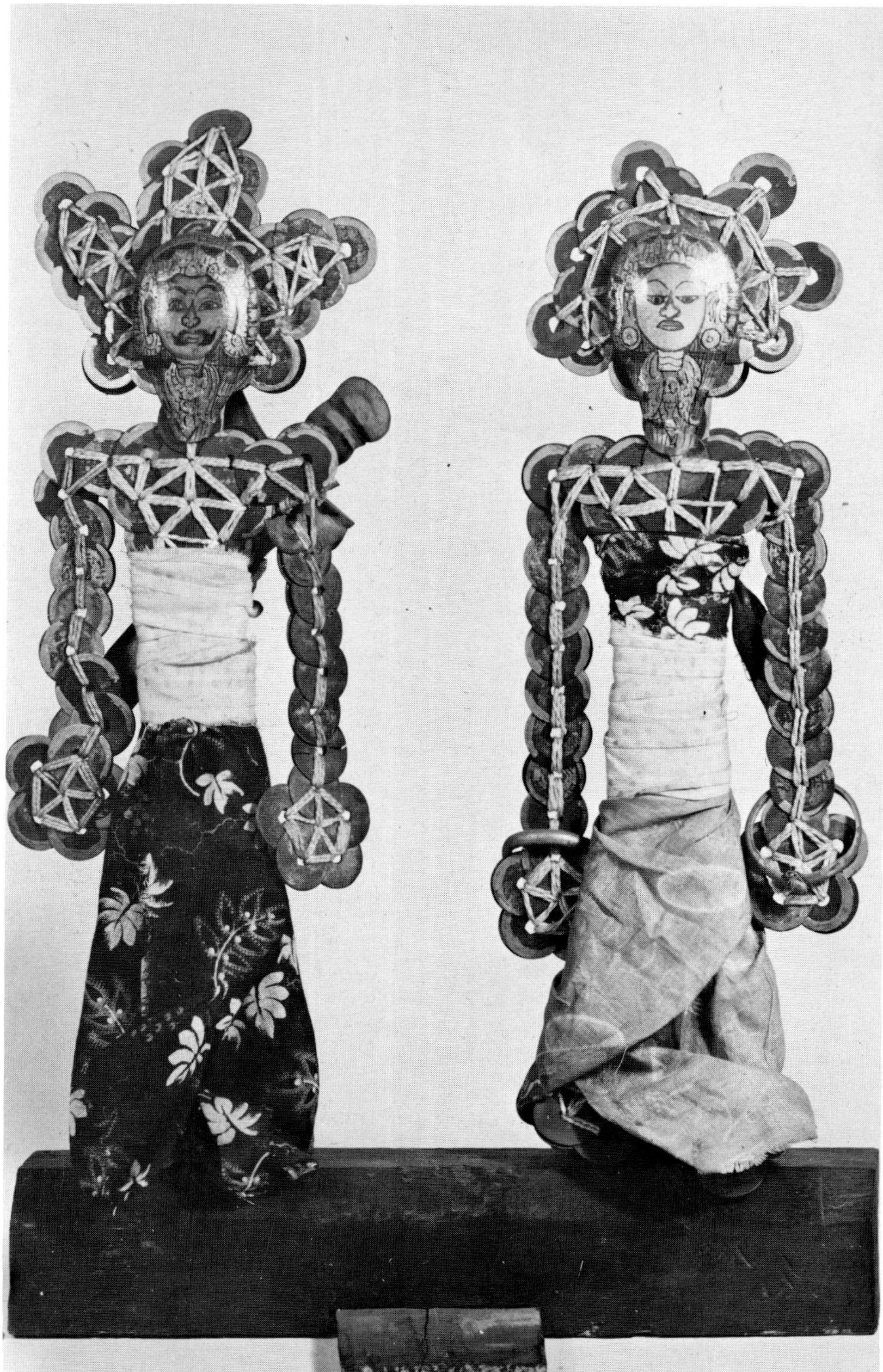

r 1

The god Sadana

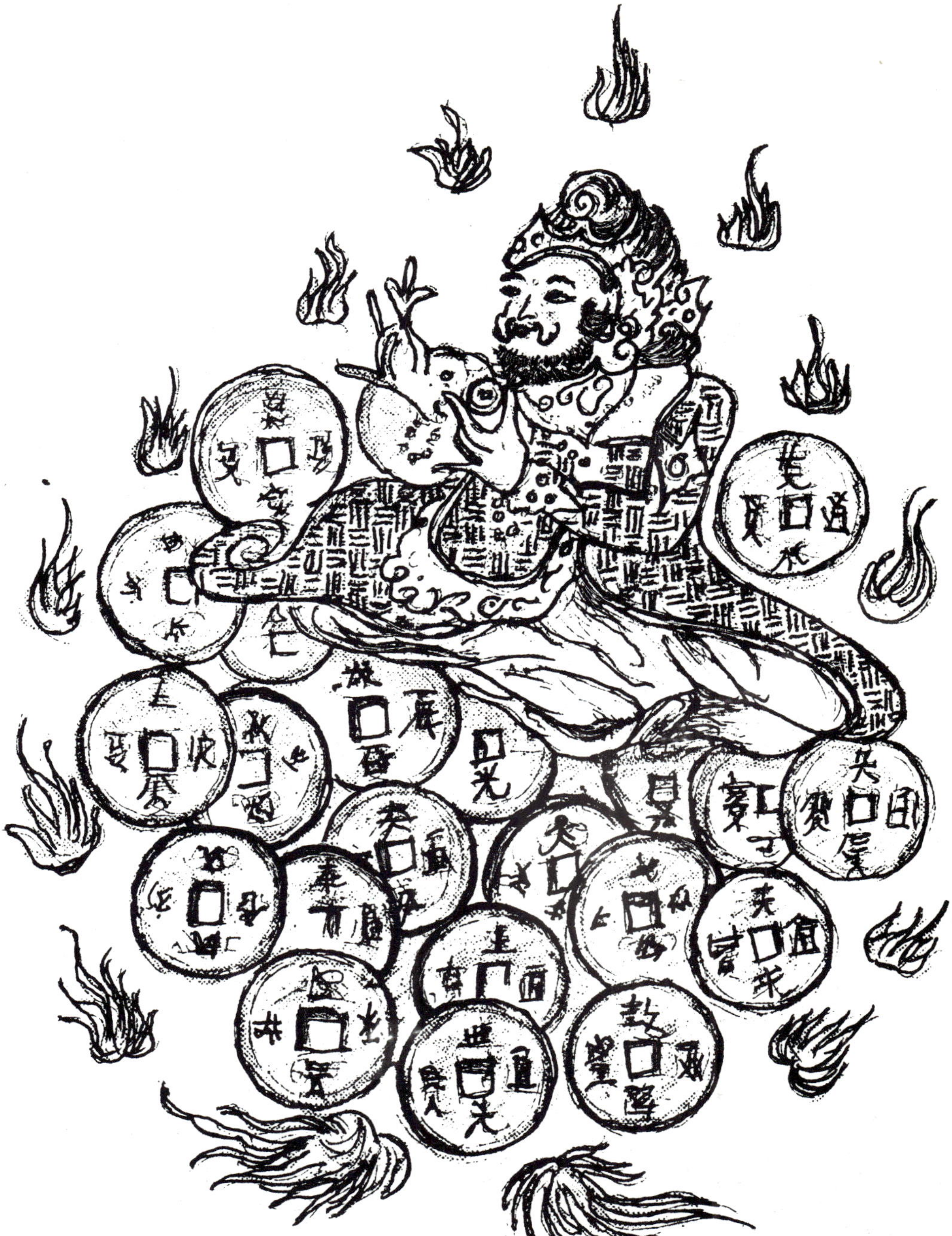

r 2

Rites de passage; 3 × 5 × 7 days of age

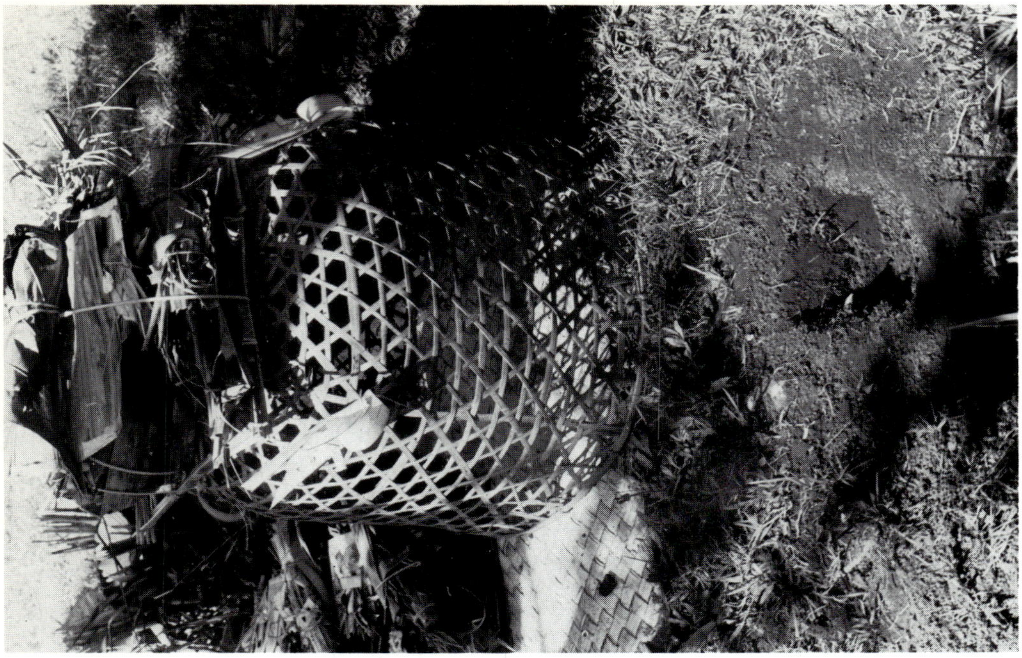

s 2

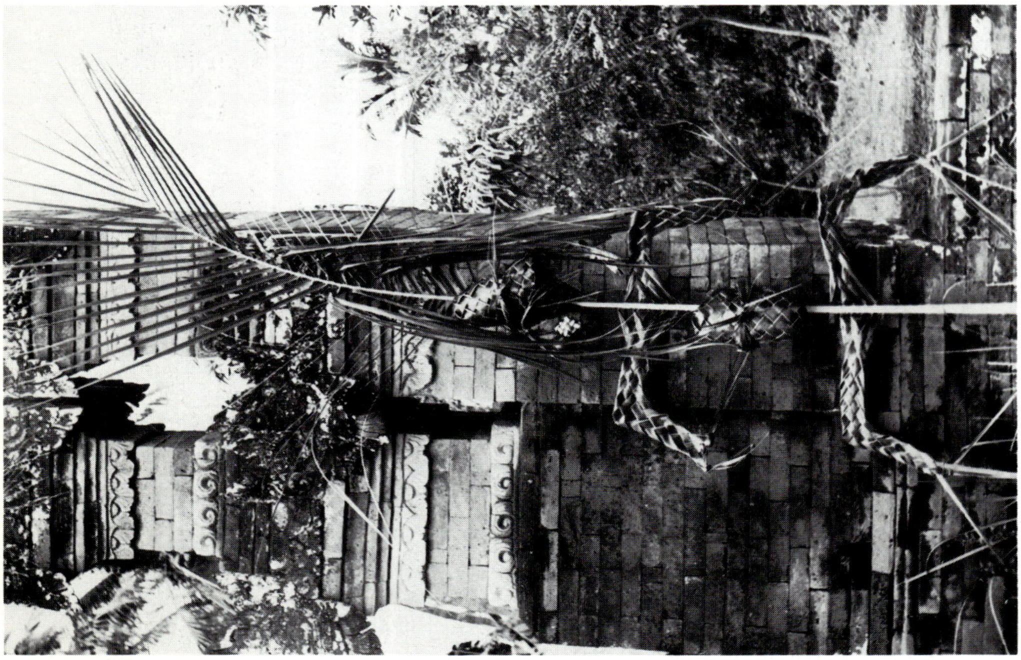

s 1

Rites de passage; 3 × 5 × 7 days of age

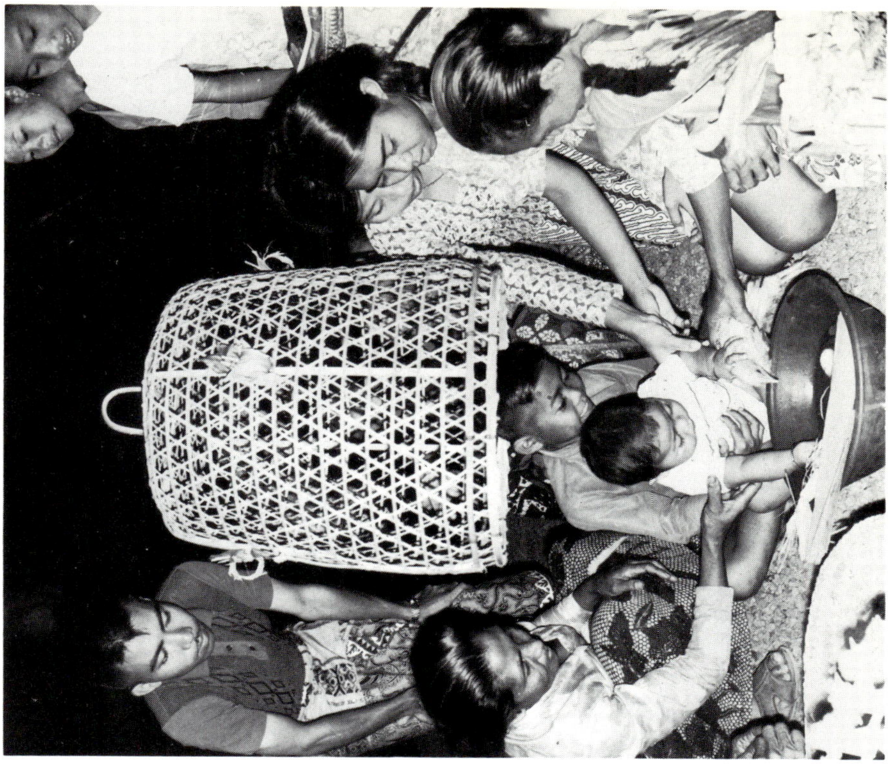

s 4

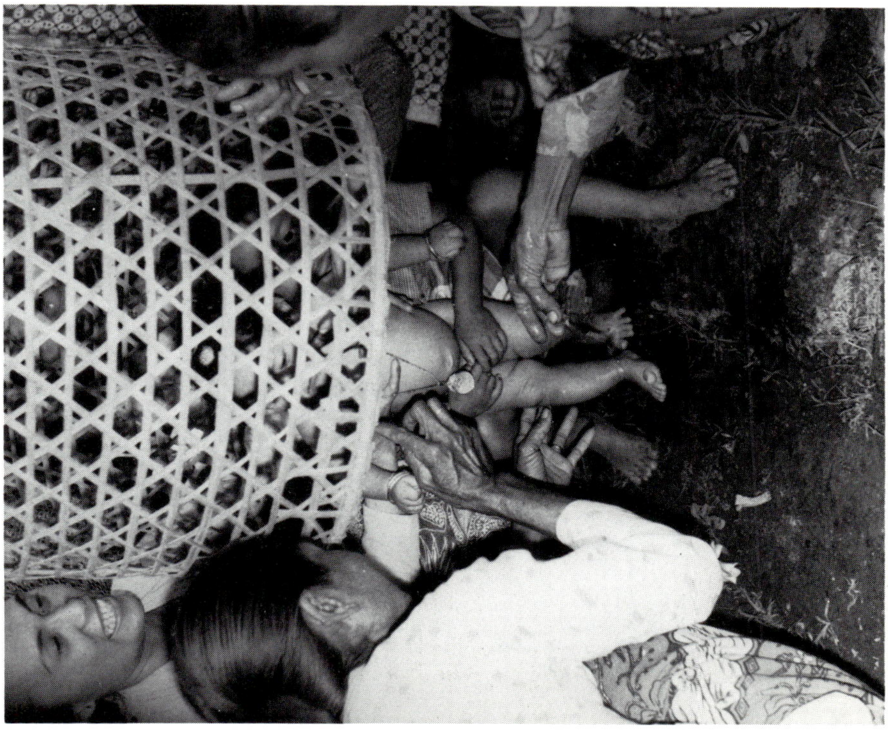

s 3

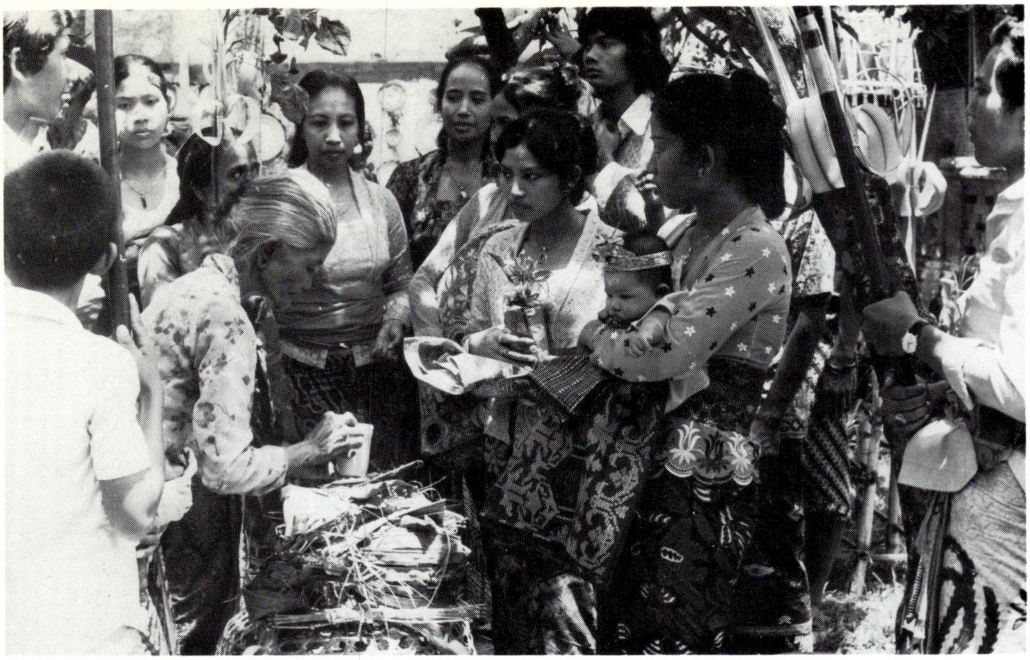

t 1

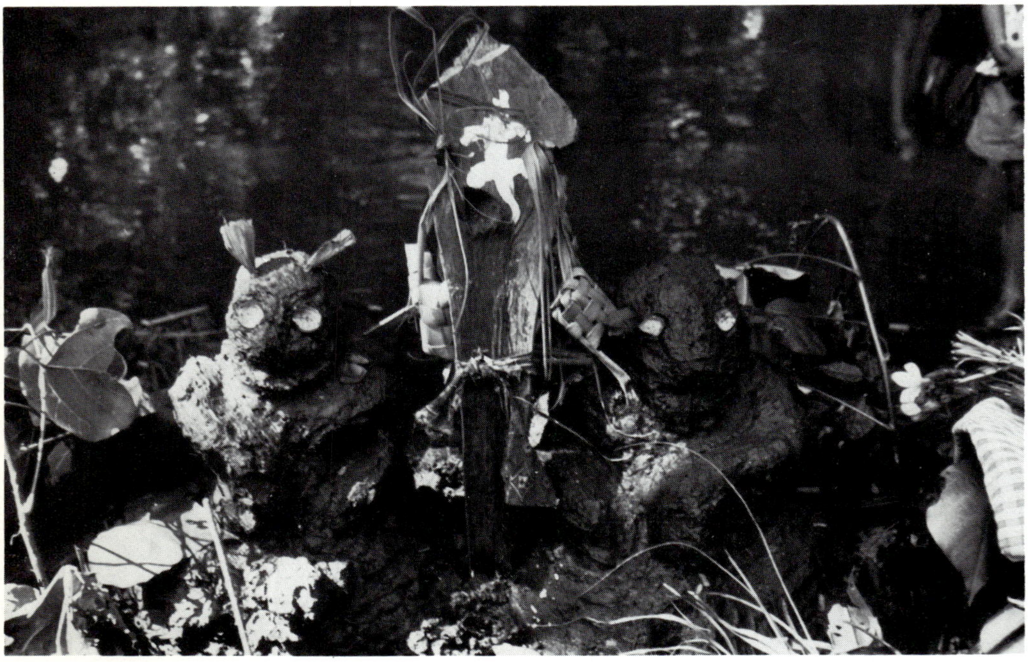

t 2

Ritual first hair-cut

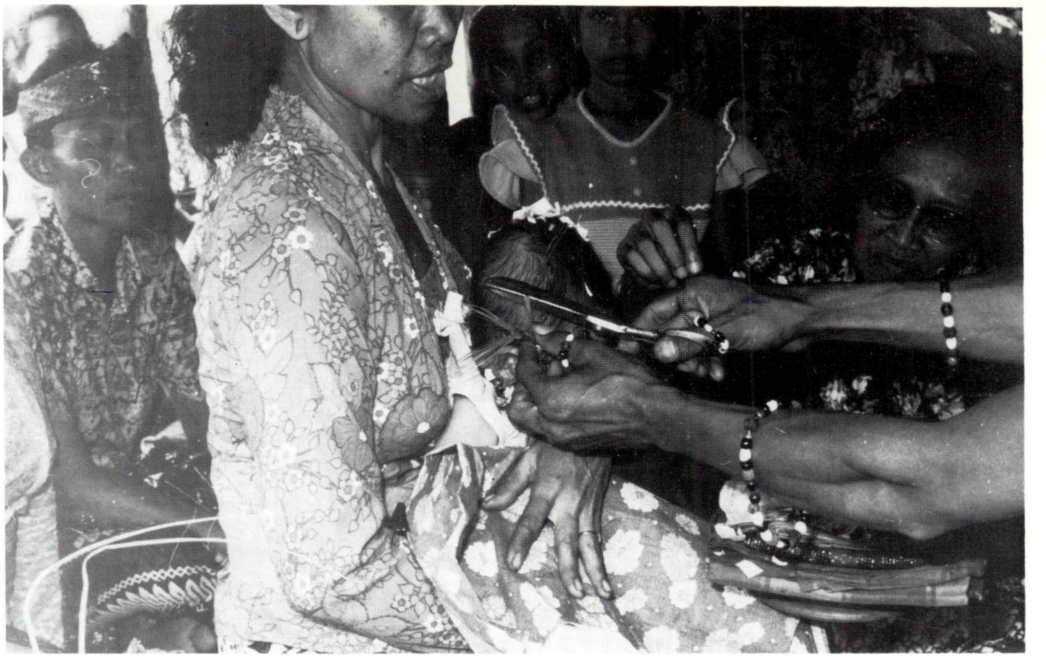

t 3

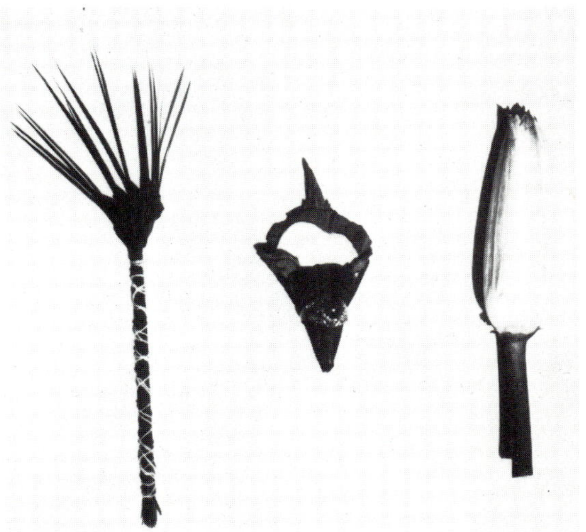

t 4

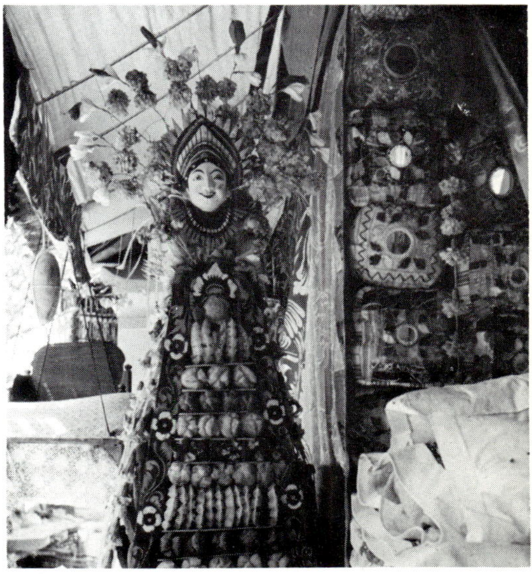

t 5

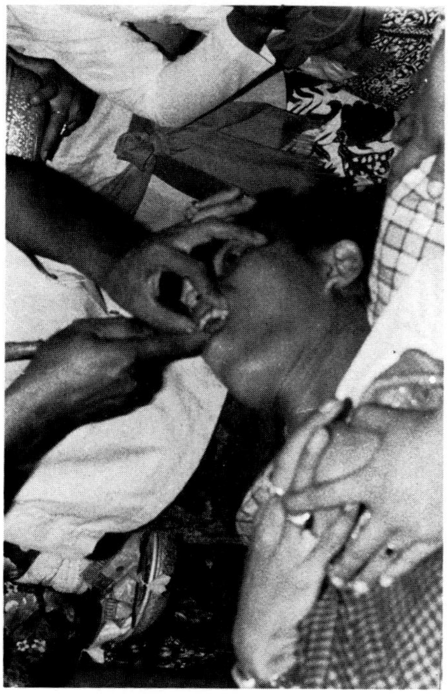

u 2

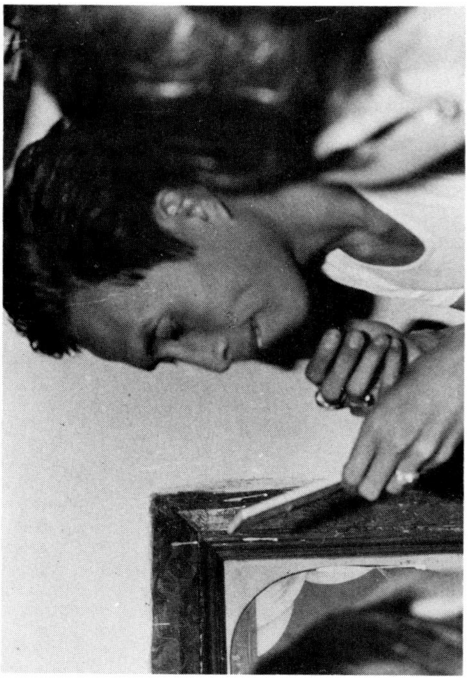

u 3

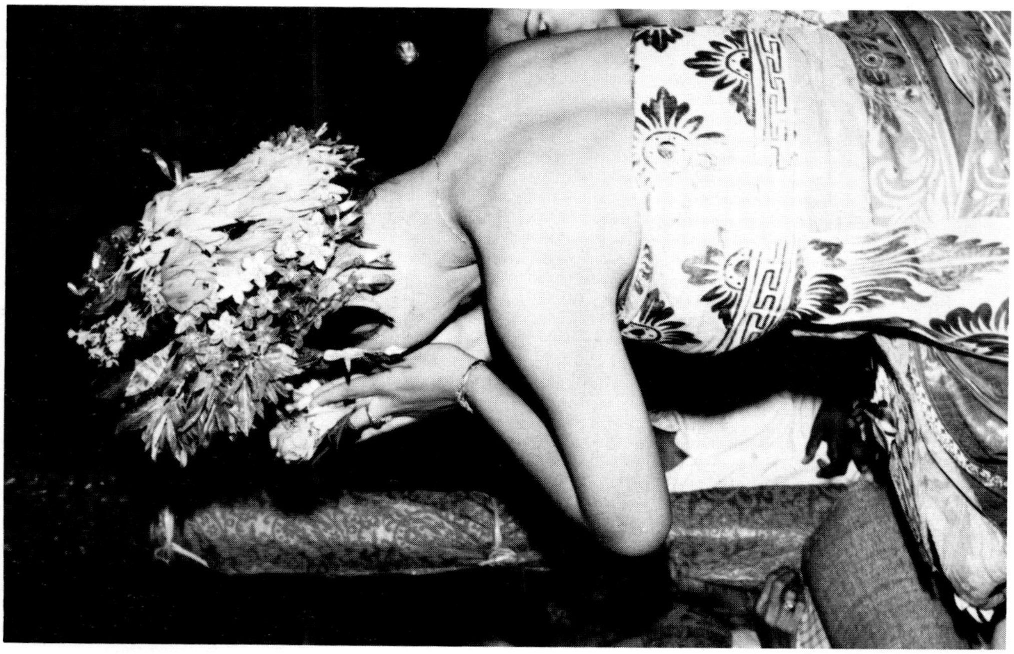

u 1

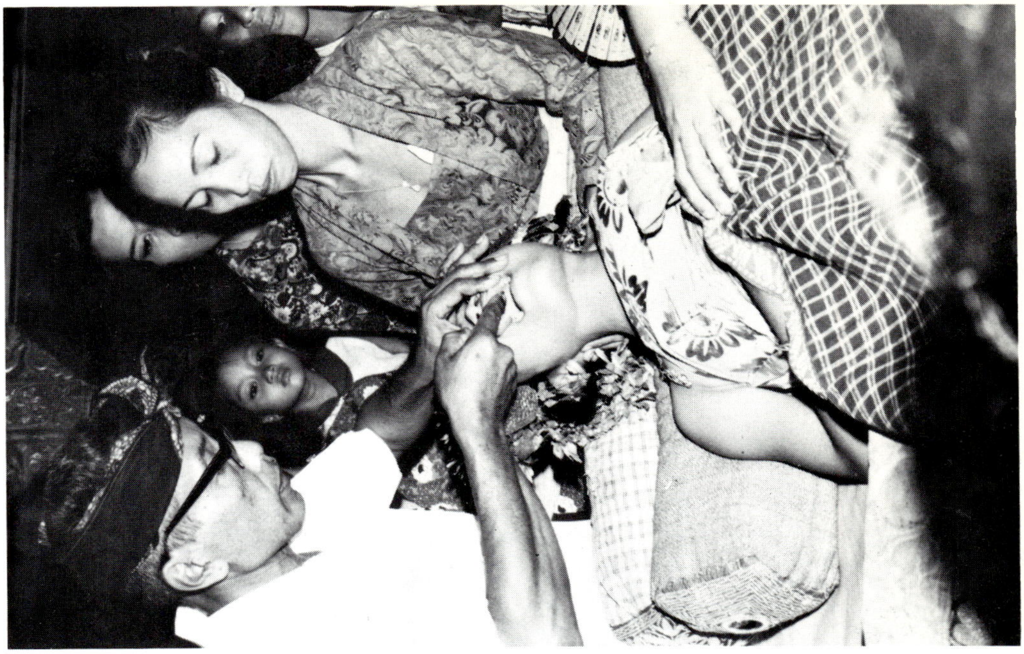

u 5

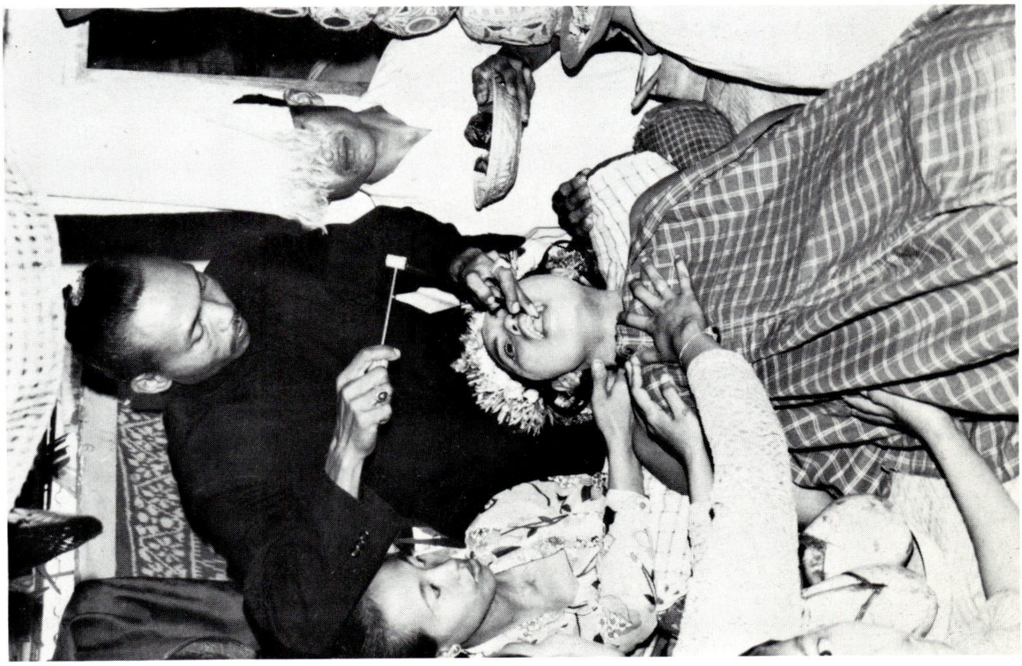

u 4

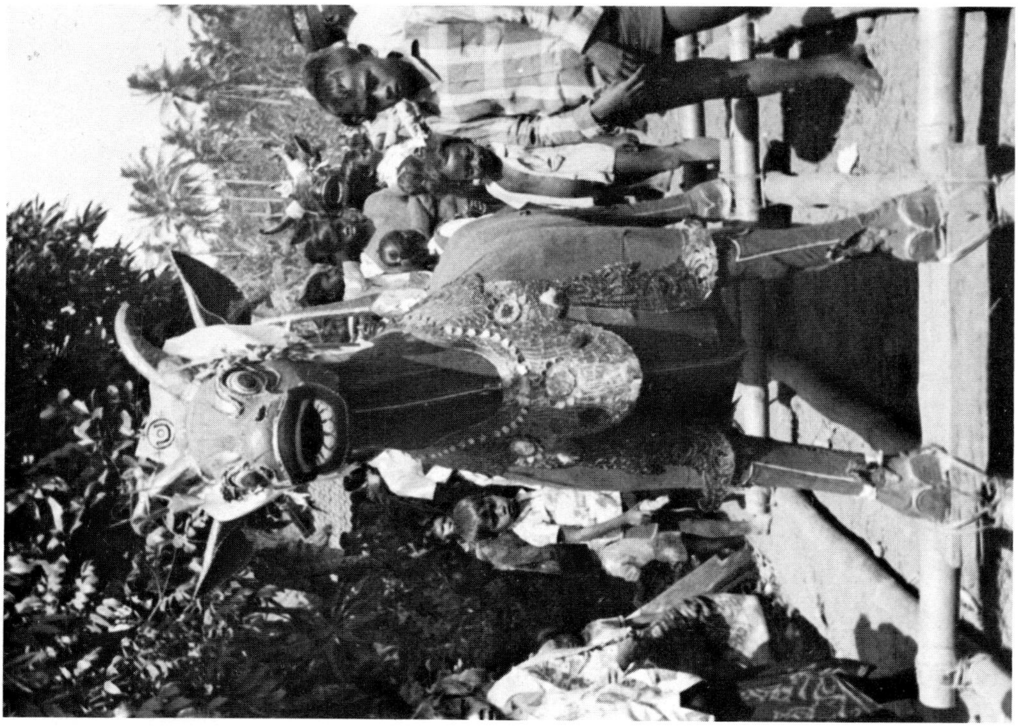

v 2

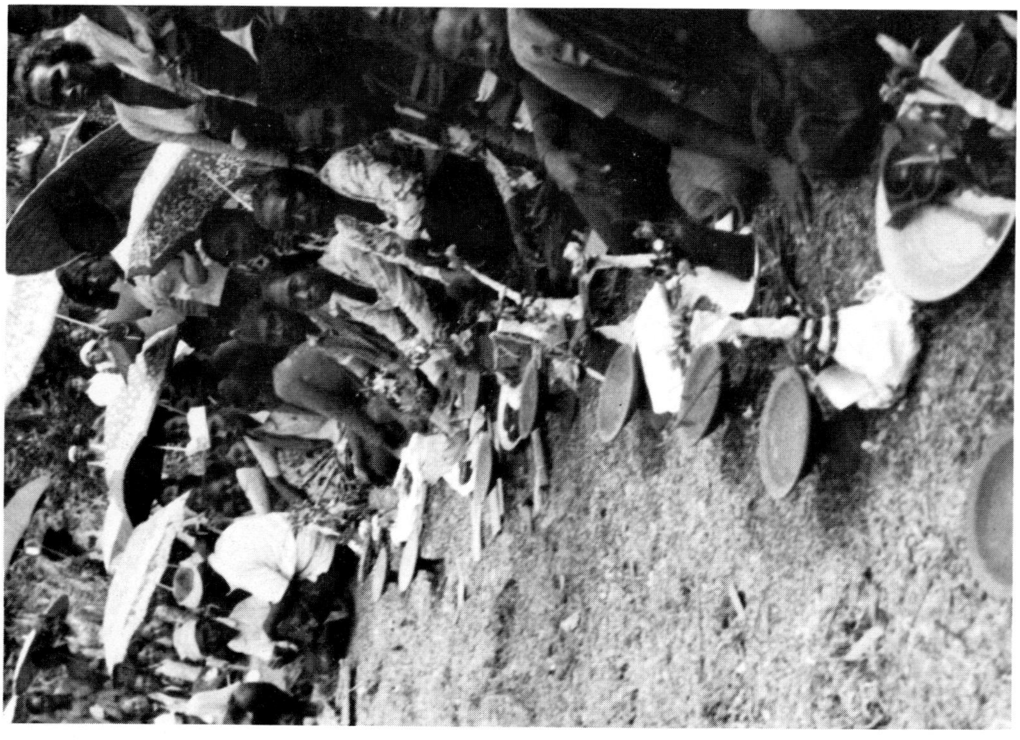

v 1

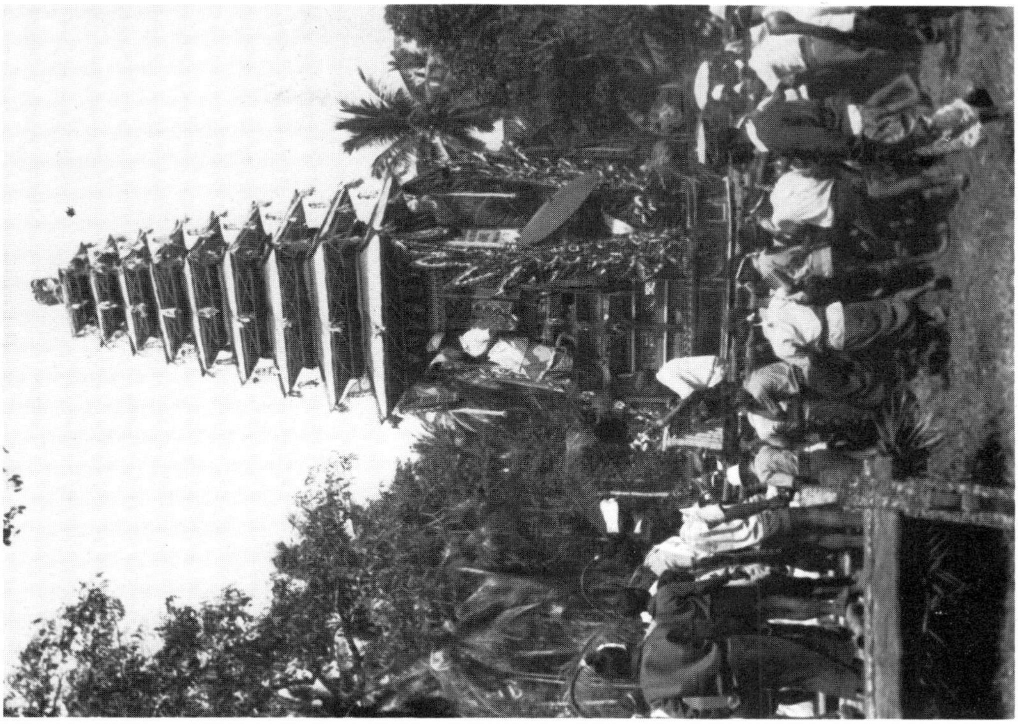

v 4

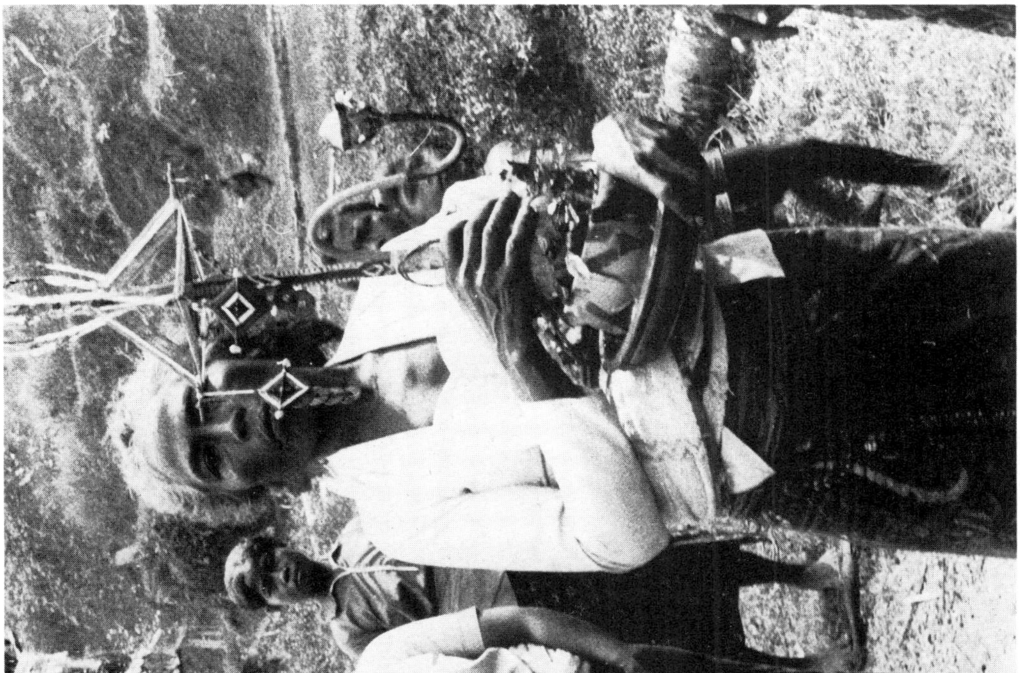

v 3

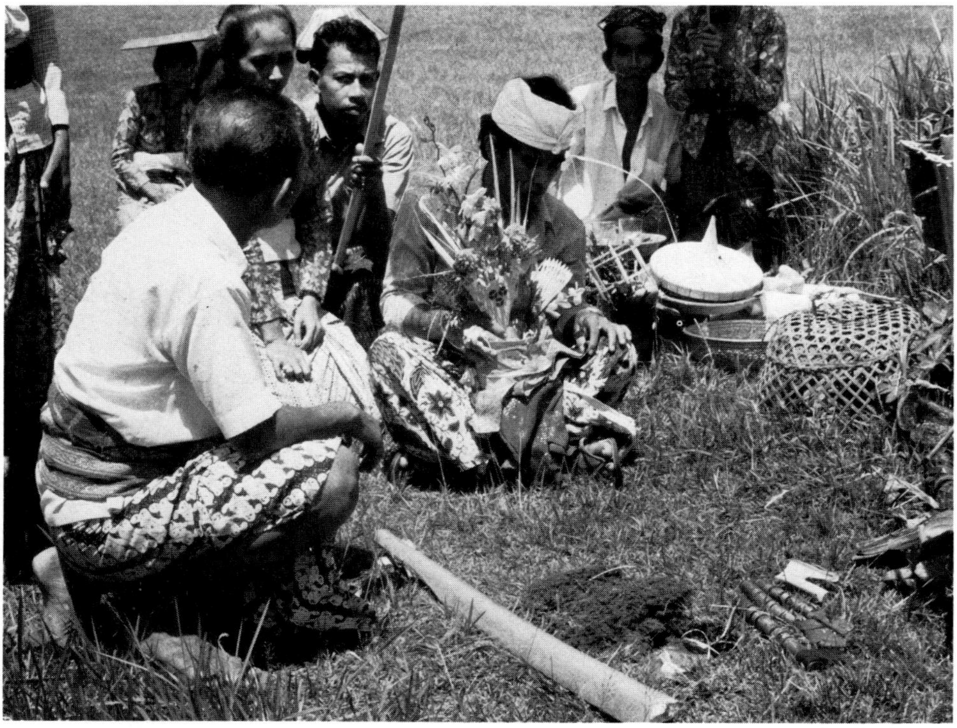

w 1

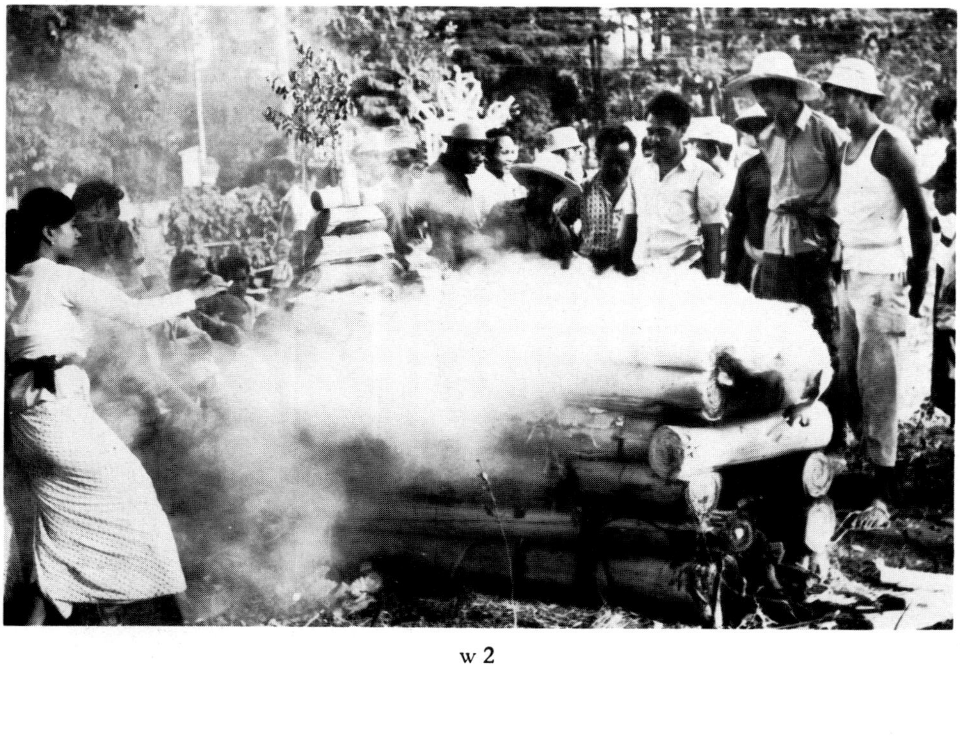

w 2

Care of the dead

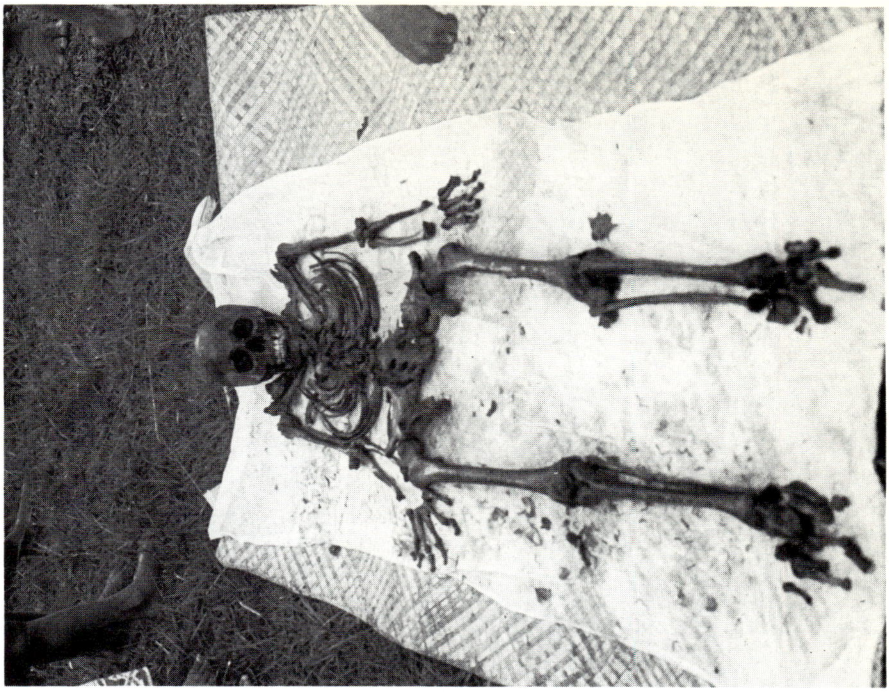

w 4

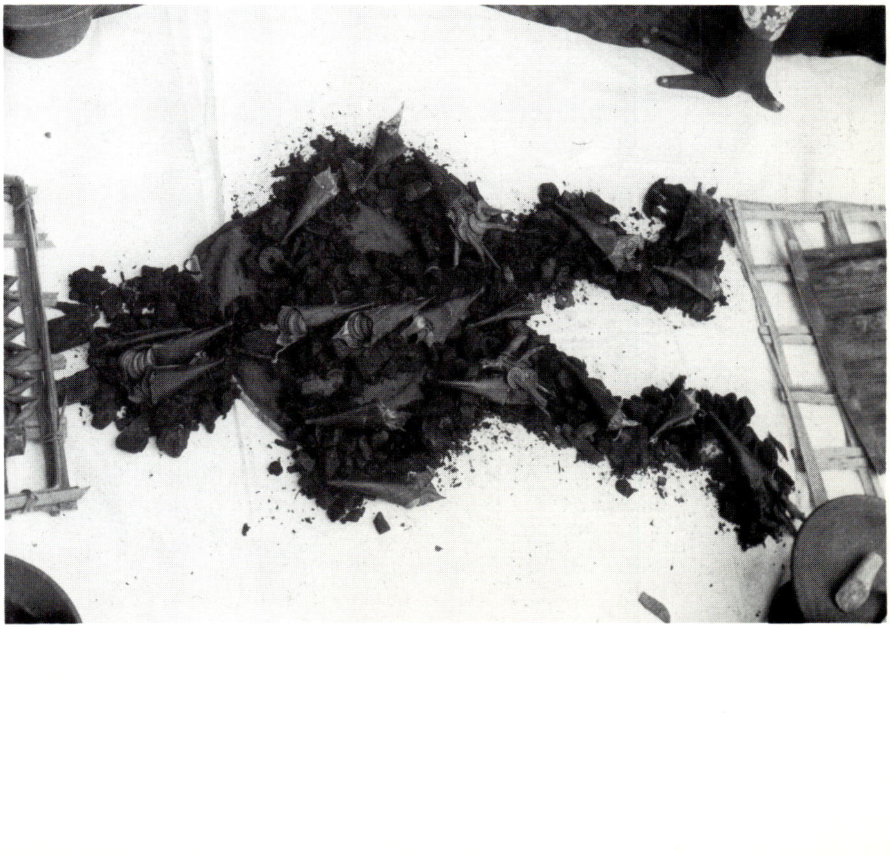

w 3

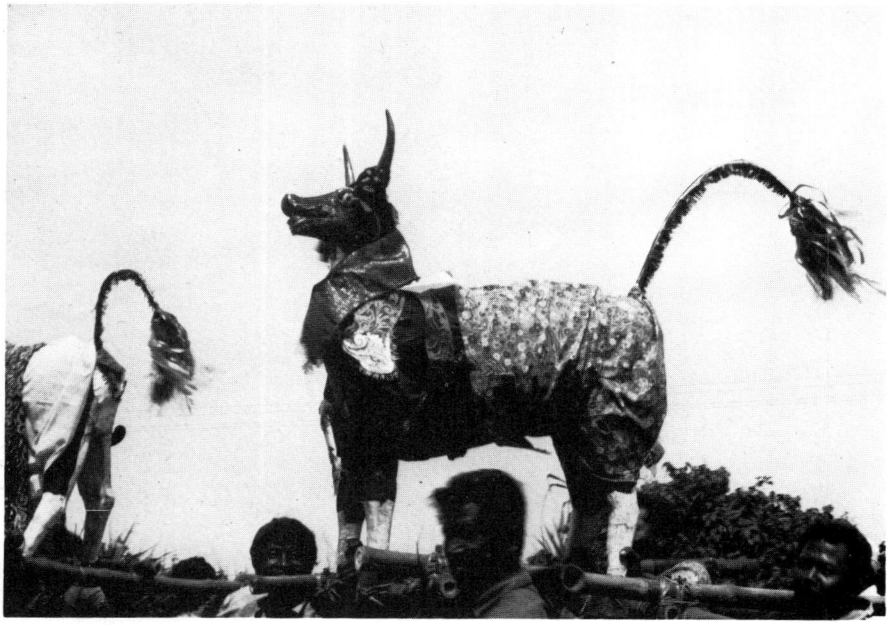

x 1

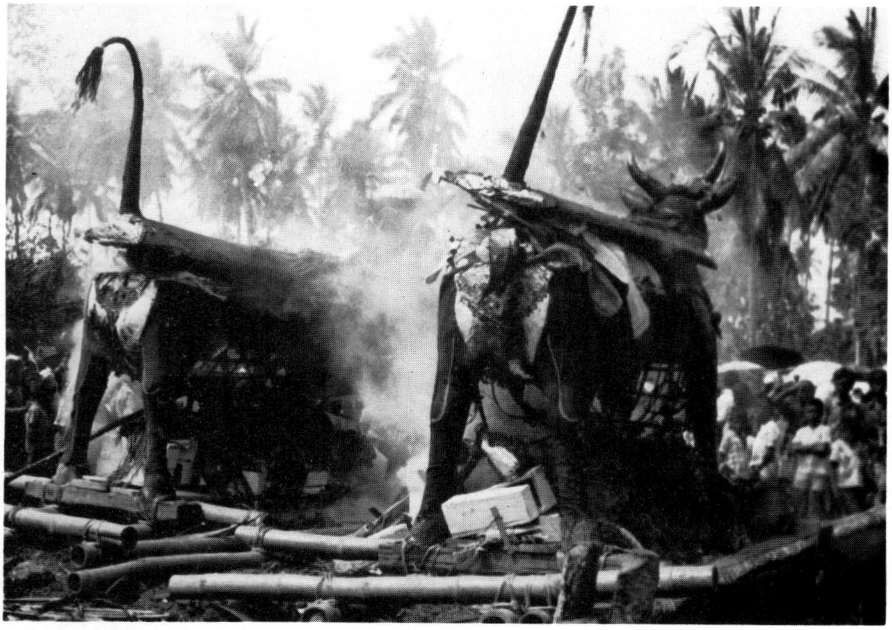

x 2

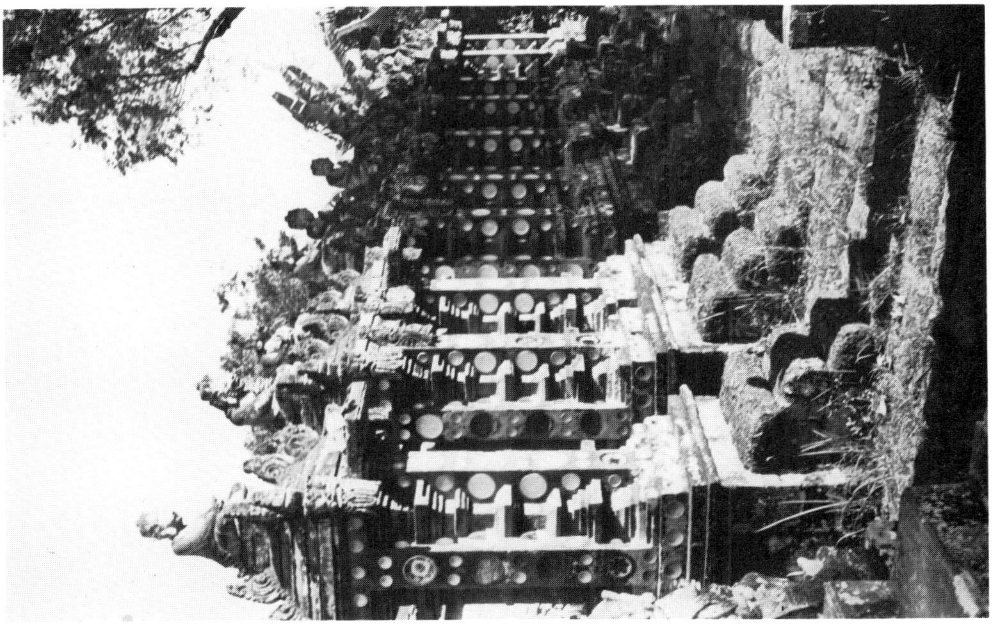

x 4

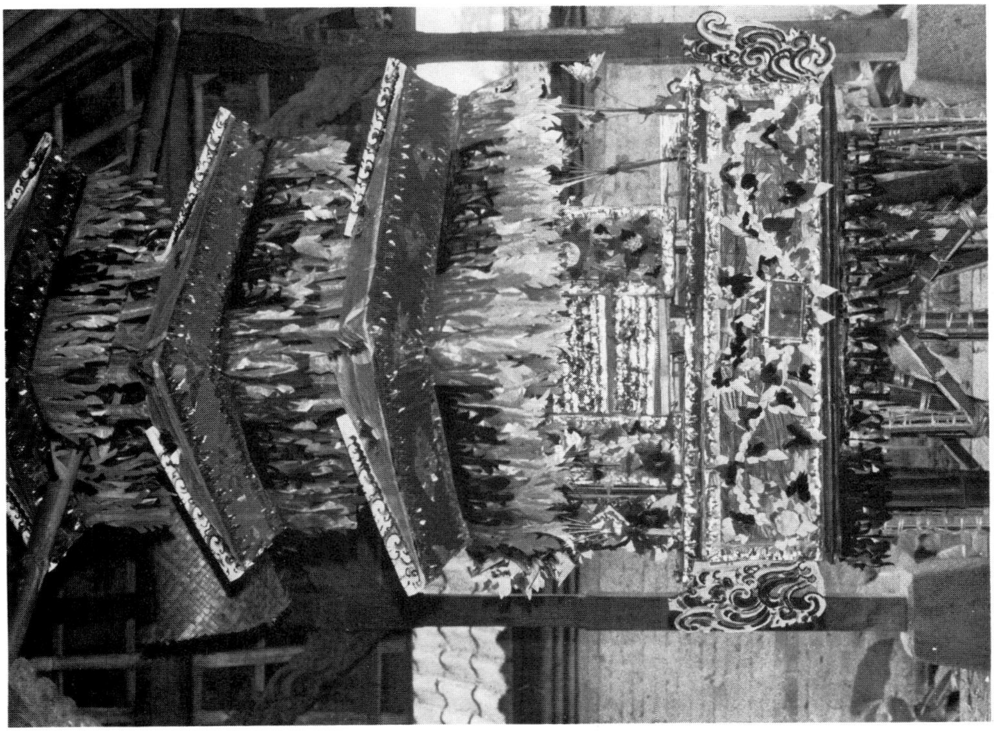

x 3

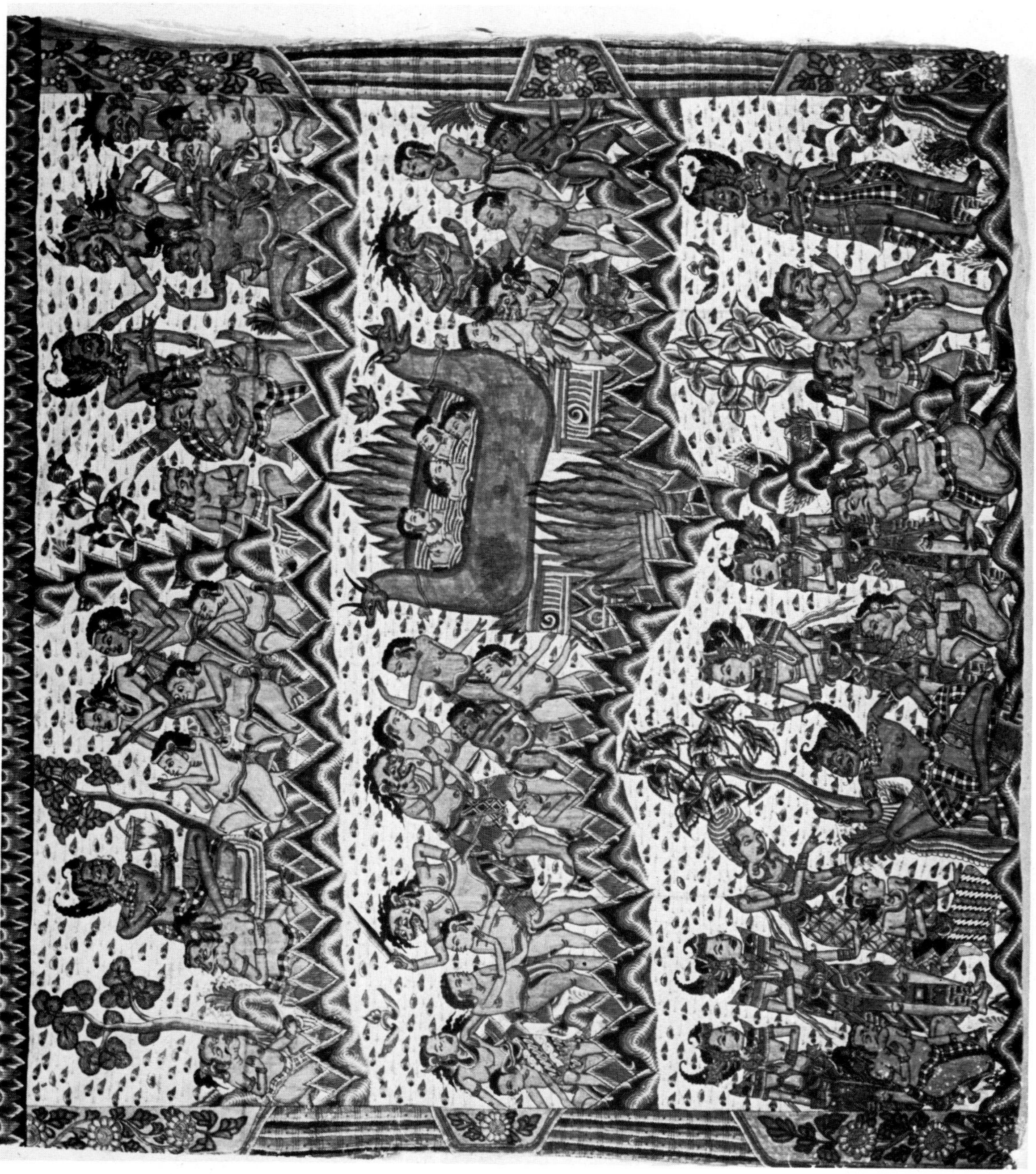

y 1

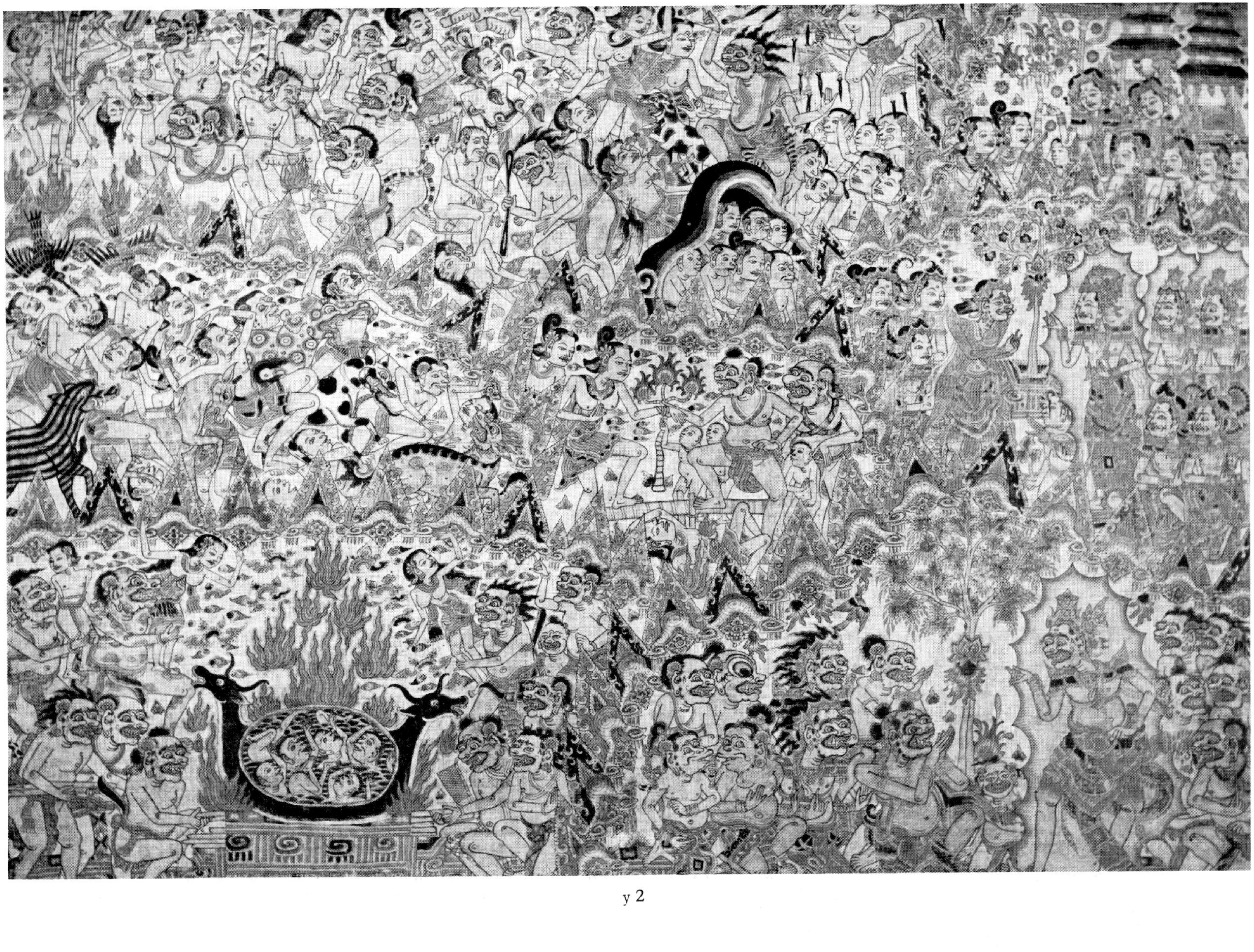

y 2

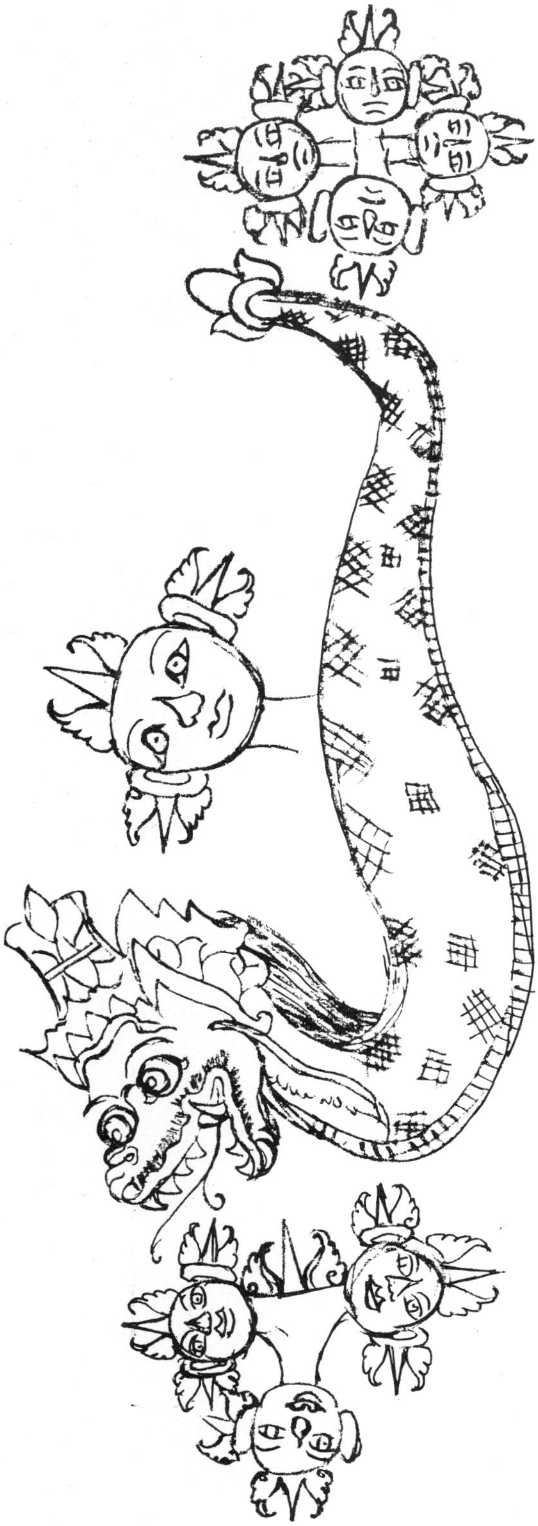

z 1

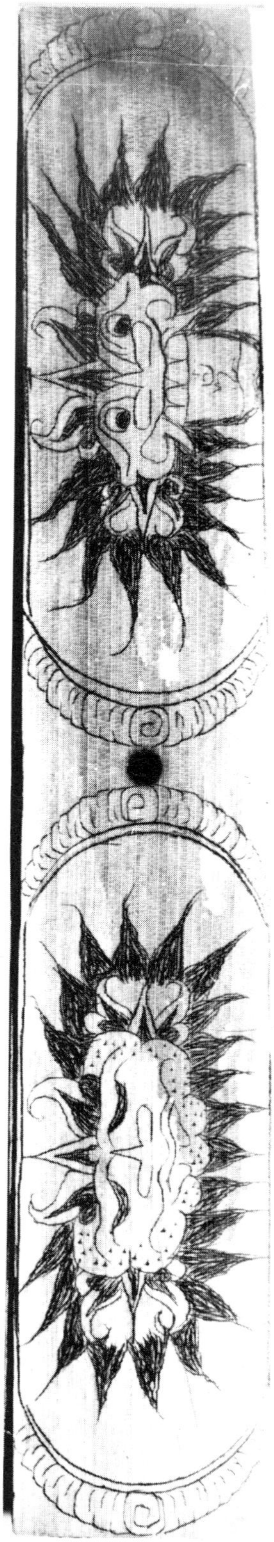

z 2